Praise for *Soul Proprietor*

A serious book that is also great fun to read. I found it to be helpful, interesting and incredibly informative.I believe that anyone in business for themselves, or just starting a business, will find this book valuable.

—Carol Duvall, Weller Grossman Productions

This powerful, practical, helpful book shows you how to achieve your entrepreneurial goals faster than you can imagine.

—Brian Tracy, Consultant, Brian Tracy International

If I'd only read this book when I was first launching my business, I could have been spared so many of the ups and downs of owning and growing my business. It's the blueprint for starting and succeeding in business.

—Nancy Michaels, President, Impression Impact

As an entrepreneur, staying true to yourself is very difficult, and nobody knows how to do it better than Jane Pollak. Read her book, and you will learn step by step how to build a business you can be proud of—a business that reflects your priorities, your values, and your unique view of the world.

—Brad Fisher, owner, 10X Partners

It's so readable, so down to earth, so chock full of sense.

—Father Paul Keenan, author of *Heartstorming*

SOUL PROPRIETOR

101 Lessons from
a Lifestyle Entrepreneur

JANE POLLAK

THE CROSSING PRESS
FREEDOM, CALIFORNIA

Copyright © 2001 by Jane Pollak
Cover and interior design by Nathan Walker
Author photo © by Lynn McCann
Printed in the U.S.A.

For information on bulk purchases or group discounts for this and other Crossing Press titles, please contact our Special Sales Director at 800/777-1048, Ext. 203.
Visit our Web site: **www.crossingpress.com**

Library of Congress Cataloging-in-Publication Data

Pollak, Jane. 1948-
    Soul proprietor : 101 lessons from a lifestyle entrepreneur / Jane Pollak.
      p. cm.
    Includes bibliographical references.
      ISBN 1-58091-108-0 (pbk.)
      1. New business enterprises--Management. 2. Women-owned business enterprises--Management 3. Home-based business--Management. 4. Small business--Management. 5. Entrepreneurship. I. Title.
    HD62.5 .P617 2001
    658'.041--dc21

                2001042254

0   9   8   7   6   5   4   3   2   1

TABLE OF CONTENTS

FOREWORD

by Peggy Kennedy
Editor-in-Chief of *Victoria* Magazine

When Jane Pollak says, "if I can make a business out of this, you can make a business out of anything!" she certainly means it. Delicate eggs painted with intricate designs that take her an average of ten hours each are not everyone's idea of a sure bet startup. This book, written with humor and from the heart, takes you through Jane's focused but daunting journey and shares the smart ideas that kept her fledgling business alive and growing.

Bringing these artistic eggs to our attention was just one step. When *Victoria* published her tour de force artworks in a beautifully photographed layout, she had an opportunity to capitalize on the publicity. But to get her business to the next level required persistence, meaningful networking, and grass-roots marketing, as well as conquering her fears and shyness. Jane turns what she learned from her ups and downs into guidelines to enlighten a novice.

Today, women own nearly half of all businesses in the United States. *Victoria* Magazine has sought out and featured unique women's businesses, many that began at home with little more than creativity and spunk. Often a woman will start a business by developing something she loves–making jam, arranging flowers, painting murals, buying and selling antiques or, as in the case of *Victoria's* latest "Entrepreneur of the Year," turning children's drawings into keepsake silver pins. Oddly enough, that talented woman introduced herself to me after an inspiring presentation by Jane Pollak at a networking night promoting one of our books. Jane's tongue-in-cheek, self-effacing enthusiasm could boost anyone's courage.

Expanding into a billion-dollar enterprise is rarely the goal of a woman who begins a business by following a personal passion. Not that the right combination of a good idea and determination couldn't produce a significant success. Witness Elizabeth Arden, Donna Karan, or Elsa Peretti. Having a strong point-of-view helps, whether it involves the perfect chocolate chip cookie or silver jewelry based on the organic forms of nature—not to mention an exquisitely painted egg!

Jane Pollak's personal path provides lessons and encouragement for anyone with a big idea for a small business. Use her tips as a template for your own success.

INTRODUCTION

I don't think my father had egg decorating in mind when he gave me advice at the breakfast table: "No matter what you decide to do with your life, be the best in your field." I have always taken his advice to heart. I grew up wanting to be an art teacher. Most women brought up in the '50s aspired to be teachers, nurses, secretaries, housewives, and mothers. Of course, that all got turned around by 1970 when better opportunities began to emerge for women of my generation. I still was on track to become a teacher, but as a studio art and theater major I planted other seeds for my career. When I finished graduate school and was hired as a high school art and stagecraft teacher, I came away with a lifelong gift. At graduate school I met Buddy Pollak, and while I was teaching, I learned the craft of Ukrainian Easter egg decorating. I fell in love with both. Buddy and I were married in 1972 and celebrated our twenty-ninth anniversary in 2001. And I have continued waxing and dyeing eggs in the Ukrainian tradition to this day. I had my first craft show in 1973 when I exhibited my decorated eggs.

I quit teaching after my first child was born in 1974 and dived into full-time mothering. I did however participate in one or two exhibits a year and taught some adult education courses. But my children have been and still are my greatest source of pride and my greatest achievement. Raising them taught me lessons no business school was capable of.

By the time my youngest child entered kindergarten in 1987 and I was somewhat freer, I had received an invitation from the White House to design an egg for their Easter Egg Roll, and I had my first one-woman show. My business education began in 1989 when I took a course for women who owned their own businesses. Over the years I have taken similar courses and joined groups like the Entrepreneurial Women's Network which gave me the chance to hear other women's experiences.

By this time I had been decorating eggs for nearly twenty years and had become an expert. A publisher consequently asked me for a book about my work. *Decorating Eggs: Exquisite Designs with Wax & Dye* was published in 1996 and is currently in its sixth printing. I now had a platform from which to address an audience and had turned a passion into a thriving business.

The above history of my life and business is what the world at large sees. However, there's another story to tell. When I was a kid, I was a crybaby. And for years I tried to cover up my hurt feelings with ice cream and unsatisfactory relationships. But both devices stopped working when I turned forty and found myself feeling the pain I had avoided for so long.

Jim Rohn said it succinctly, " Work harder on yourself than you do on your career." I followed his advice and took the time to examine my fundamental belief system. It was comprised of three whining statements: It shouldn't be this hard; I shouldn't have to do this; this shouldn't be happening. I made the decision to discard this belief system and build a new one from scratch. I got help from recovery work, therapy, and experiential workshops. Since 1989 I have been exploring, uncovering, and revising the messages of my past while carrying on an increasingly successful business.

From day one my ambition has been to earn money doing the work I love, and to have time for my family and friends, and especially time for myself. My decisions now come from my heart and gut rather than from my calculator. I know that my feelings of self-worth are really more important than how I set the list prices for my work. One day at a time I face the challenges of being an entrepreneur and listen to my heart and soul for the proper solutions.

CHAPTER 1

Image

"I want to introduce you to a fabulous artist."
"Terrific! What type of art does she do?"
"She decorates eggs."
"Oh, really? Can you pass me the butter?"

Most entrepreneurs don't have the problem I have in defining who I am. Their products and services are more comprehensible to the public. I had to claw and scratch my way to get the bare minimum of professional respect. Throughout the process I have learned what it takes to create an image or brand for a business. I know that how I answer my phone, the look of my correspondence, the speed of my response time, and the eloquence of my marketing materials all convey the image of my business. In 1980 I officially became a business.

The lessons in this book apply to all entrepreneurs. Maybe you won't have to learn them the hard way, the way I did.

LESSON 1

Take care of your image,
and you will be taken seriously.

Throughout my career I have been confronted with something common to legions of women who own their own businesses—not being taken seriously. For example, back in the mid 1970s, I taught my first adult education course. At a faculty gathering before the semester started I was seated next to a man who asked what I was going to teach. He was offering a course in financial planning. When I told him I was going to teach quilting, he looked at me quizzically and asked, "Is there a book in that?" He doubted that there was enough content in the subject for a semester's worth of classes. My first thought was how little he knew. Then it occurred me that he, like many other people, didn't know that quilting was an old American art form that was now becoming popular again. Finally I realized that I was really upset because he put me down—by the way he simply dismissed me as a teacher. It took me that long to know he was insulting me.

Another time, a salesman stopped by my house to deliver an order. He looked around and remarked, "Oh, you really are a business." Because my office was in my house, he had predetermined I was not really a business person. A phone technician once spent hours doing the wiring for the dedicated business and fax lines in my renovated studio. While he attended to his job, I applied wax and dye patterns to eggs for an upcoming event. I noticed him glancing at me every few minutes wondering what I was doing. After I showed him the process of decorating eggs at different stages, he was puzzled, "Is that really your job?"

It has taken me years to feel comfortable explaining what I do to people. Most often when I say I am an artist and my medium is Ukrainian Easter eggs, the response is patronizing. I do more than just decorate eggs. Even when I first put my wares out to sell—when even I didn't know it would turn into a career—I was conscious that the public really didn't accept the fact that anyone could make a business out of egg decorating.

I realized then that it would be up to me to establish the seriousness of my enterprise. My role model is my friend Linda Carr—a doll maker and best-selling designer for Vogue Patterns.

She knows how successful she's been, how gifted she is, and what beautiful work she produces. She's not worried about how she is perceived. She's not compelled to explain the breadth of her business. It is enough for people to appreciate the wonders she has brought to our world.

L E S S O N   2

If you really want something, pursue it directly.

Jealousy has often fueled my entrepreneurial fires. I subscribed to an elegant periodical called Ornament, which highlights handmade articles of clothing, jewelry, and other collectibles. They have a monthly page dedicated to one artist, featuring photographs of the artist's work, as well as a personal statement. Typically, when I come across features like this I think, how do you get that magazine's attention? How do you make that kind of great exposure happen? Do you need to show up at the right exhibits with an impressive booth and goods? Does the publisher or editor have to be a fan? For months I looked at that page and drooled over its contents, jealous of the artist's good fortune in being selected.

On a whim one day, I called to find out how to get published in that magazine. I was told that any artist could submit photographs and a statement for consideration. I put together my statement, sent along a few slides, and promptly received a phone call notifying me that my statement would run in a future issue.

I did an immediate turnaround as I often do—akin to Groucho Marx who remarked that he didn't want to become a member of any club that would accept him. Once the magazine accepted me, I was not so impressed by the magazine and its contents. I recognize this attitude now as a self-protection device. If I lowered my opinion of the magazine, if I didn't get a positive response later on when my work appeared there, I wouldn't be so disappointed.

LESSON 3

Perception is everything.
Keep your message clear and consistent.

If a package comes in a brown wrapper, its origins are questionable. If it's engraved, it's pricey. If it's pink or purple, it's for women. We as consumers are trained to make judgments about every image that passes across our radar screens. Billions of dollars are spent on marketing and advertising that have taught us to evaluate products and services in a nanosecond. With information bombarding us at record levels, getting an entrepreneur's message across is a marketing challenge. I've experienced this from both ends of the spectrum—as a business owner and as a buyer of goods and services.

When I first began showing my work at craft fairs, I placed my intricately decorated eggs in whimsical settings—cradled in a bird's nest, or grouped in a porcelain bowl accessorized with a sterling silver spoon. The display did catch the attention of the crowds walking by. The eggs could be touched, even though discreetly placed signs asked onlookers to refrain from handling the work.

One day, an elderly, bespectacled woman entered my booth, inspected my display, reached her hand into the nest, lifted up three of my prettiest designs, and took out a one-dollar bill, "I'll take these." Something about the image I had created with my display must have suggested to her that my eggs were 35 cents each, not the 35 dollars each noted on the sign I had so carefully placed beside the bird's nest.

I knew that I had to alter the perception of what I was selling. The nest idea had to go. I began to exhibit my eggs in glass showcases or under glass domes, thereby informing the public that they were Art. The presentation reinforces your customer's expectation of what you are selling. I was saying that my eggs cost a lot and were worth the money.

Bulgari, one of the most expensive jewelry stores on Fifth Avenue in New York, changed its image in the opposite direction, by making their wares more accessible. Where once a guard buzzed shoppers into the store, now there was a revolving door. Where once all shoppers had to be guided to a private room by a sales clerk before they could inspect the jewelry, now all they had to do was walk in the door, look at the jewelry that was visible in glass cases and a clerk would walk over to wait on them. Bulgari management had decided their store was too intimidating for American customers.

As a consumer, I too am influenced by my perceptions. I worked with a designer from California when I created my first logo. Everything about him was buttoned-down—coolly professional. I admired his artistry as well as his business acumen. A few years later I wanted him to update the logo, but wasn't sure I had written down his e-mail address correctly. To check, I looked up his AOL member profile and got really confused. His nickname was topmanLA77. His occupation was sex, and his AOL quote was more sex. I got very nervous about using his services, but had to give him the benefit of the doubt. I called him to tell him I was a little nervous when I saw his e-mail profile and wanted to make sure I had the right address. Was he still in the same business? He assured me he was. I then asked whether he was aware of the perception he was creating with the AOL profile. He was puzzled, "What profile are you referring to?" It seemed that an employee had jokingly submitted the information. He was very surprised and corrected it immediately.

LESSON 4

The public needs to place us, and it's our job to make it easy for them.

Before entering the craft show market, I visited my first craft fair and saw a woman who sold decorated eggs. They weren't anything like mine, so I didn't regard her as competition, but I hated her moniker, The Egg Lady. It sounded cheap and Humpty-Dumptyish. I gave my business a fancier name, An Egg by Jane. It was simple, direct, and you knew what you were getting. I've carried that name with me for over twenty years and it's been successful. However, there's a down side I can't avoid. No matter where I display my work, from the most sophisticated craft soirees to corporate lunchrooms, I keep being referred to as the egg lady. It's simply how people remember me. I used to cringe when I heard it, but now I know it's better to be remembered as the egg lady than not to be remembered at all.

Later on I spoke at an inventors' club, along with a man who talked about his newly conceived gadget for bird watchers. I didn't know his name and simply called him the bird guy. When the phrase slipped right of my mouth, I began to laugh at my own need to put someone into a box where I could remember him.

I once attended a lecture by Thomas Mann, a talented, successful, and innovative designer of jewelry. He said that he is "happily stuck in techno-romantic," a category he created and built a business on. Today, I am equally happily stuck as the egg lady. In fact, I now own the toll-free number 877 EGG LADY.

It's best to focus your message carefully
in every aspect of your business—
written, visual, and operational

Maybe because I was a child of the free-spirited '60s, I resisted creating an identity for my business. I was an artist, free to create whatever I wanted, whenever I wanted. However, once I decided I was going to make a business out of my art, that rationale began to pale. I began to recognize the need to project a consistent message about who I was and what I could offer. Even though I named my company An Egg by Jane, once I allowed myself to be called the egg lady. I had taken the first step in becoming the owner of a business.

I hired a graphic artist to design my first brochure. Because I had a small budget, she suggested that I select a limited number of eggs to feature and then organize them so that my customers could see everything I had to offer. How could I eliminate that one-of-a-kind gem that someone somewhere was dying to own? Probably my reaction came from my deep insecurity that perhaps people would see nothing they liked in an edited version of the brochure and therefore would not buy anything. The designer helped me realize that tailoring the message increases the customer's understanding of what's being offered and makes the selection easier. But tailoring goes beyond brochures. In addition to what I put in print for the world to see, I, as the proprietor, carry the brand of my business daily.

I'll never forget my disappointment when I went to show my work to a museum curator and entered a small, cluttered office with thousands of dollars worth of merchandise gathering dust on her overcrowded shelves. What seemed so elegant in the museum shop's sparkling cases looked like tag sale leftovers. It made me realize how important image is, how one is perceived. The New York Times addressed the subject of image in an article about dentists. They stressed that even the dentist's pen counted in the patient's perception.

LESSON 6

It's necessary to dress the part.

"Your haircut is too suburban," the image consultant informed me. She taught the final session in a semester-long course for women who owned their own businesses. It was a wise move on her part to save this session for last. We students had grown comfortable with each other and understood exactly what each person needed to communicate to her marketplace. One by one, we took our turn in front of the class to learn how we might improve our visual message. The accountant who wanted to attract a more creative clientele was advised to trade in her conservative navy suit for more stylish dresses and statement jewelry. No more tiny stud earrings. Chunky clip-ons would complete her look. The computer consultant was advised to cut off her ponytail. It conveyed a negative message to corporate clients. When it was my turn, the instructor asked me what image I would like to convey. "Artistic, sophisticated, stylish," I responded. After assessing me, she recommended a New York hair stylist as well as an outlet for designer clothing.

Our class had a reunion six months after that final session. What a delight to witness the transformations! Our accountant not only looked more creative and well accessorized, she also reported that her business was taking off by leaps and bounds with precisely the clients she had hoped to attract. The computer consultant had changed her hairdo and was successfully working with a number of corporate customers. Everyone loved my asymmetrical haircut and chic new outfit. I, too, had begun to feel more like the contemporary craft artist I wanted to be. Image is not the solution to everything, but dressing the part to support your work is a step toward business success.

L E S S O N 7

If you're going to compete in business,
your printed materials need to project
the statement that you are a serious player.

At one of my marketing seminars, a man asked me what I thought
about his flier. With some hesitation and tact I told him that his flier
looked as though he had printed it in his basement. He was proud to
admit it. "I did do it in my basement—on my own copier." He had
missed my point. It's important to project the image that you're serious
about your business. Nobody wants to know that you printed your
material in your basement. All it does is broadcast what league you're
playing in.

I found I had to upgrade the look and feel of my marketing materials to enter a bigger league. I had an elegant logo created that would
reach a more sophisticated audience than I had previously targeted, but
my written materials did not match that upscale look. I knew I needed
help conveying something about me and my products that I was unable
to articulate. Through a referral I met Marci Levin, a gifted copywriter.
She spent the first part of our first meeting asking me about my business and reviewing my work and marketing materials. She appreciated
the delicacy of my handwork and the uniqueness of my business. As
soon as she said that she was going to create a romance around my
eggs, I knew I was in the right hands. I could never have come up with
the word, but when she said it, I knew exactly what she meant—and
couldn't wait for her to do that for my business.

Marci created several marketing pieces for me, starting with an insert in my brochure entitled "The Opulent Egg." She wrote about "the timeless paisleys, classic Egyptian motifs, exquisite Ukrainian patterns—the world of vivid color and intricate design that is AN EGG BY JANE." That's romance! I loved what she wrote, believed it to be true, but could never have produced those words myself. I was too modest. Hiring Marci was the beginning of allowing other creative people to describe, illustrate, and promote my work. Their expertise gave me a much bigger image than if I had continued promoting myself. I was able to take a backseat to their talents and allow them to shape an image that would capture a wider audience.

The bonus of having a great copywriter has been twofold. The mental and emotional time it would have taken me to create those marketing messages is now devoted to doing what I do best—creating my products—and living up to these marketing messages. I am becoming, more and more, the creator of opulent eggs.

L E S S O N 8

Words shape your company's image. Make sure they reflect what you want said about your business.

"I liked that little speech you gave," a man in the audience praised Dr. Julie White. She looked at him and smiled, "Oh, that. That was my jumbo speech." It was a memorable example of how you can gently correct a fan whose intention is to compliment you. Words are such an important part of how we characterize ourselves and what we do. They shape how the world views our enterprise, and upon repetition, they form our self-image regarding our company. I've taught myself to eliminate words like just and little. Part of our job is to edit our words so that they reflect what we want to have said about our businesses.

I often think about how others minimize what we do. It's up to me to gently correct their perception and reinforce my self-worth at the same time. A friend of mine pointed out my handmade earrings to her mother, who admired them and said sincerely, "How nice that you have such a practical hobby." With kindness and affection, I let her know that my jewelry was not a hobby. It was a career and livelihood.

LESSON 9

Get as much mileage as you can from opportunities that arise, but keep it honest.

After ten years of operating my business in Connecticut, I heard about an organization called the Entrepreneurial Woman's Network and was impressed when I found out its headquarters were in a high-priced commercial location on the gold coast of Fairfield County. I wanted to learn more about the association, so I got in the car one morning to check them out. But rather than the office complex I was anticipating, I saw only a small, New England-style building with a sign out front that read, "Mail Boxes Etc." Having never heard of this company—this was 1989, long before Mail Boxes Etc. had popped up on every block—I went inside to find out if EWN had moved its location. "Oh, no. They're right over there in Suite 646," explained the proprietor, pointing to a 3" x 6" mail receptacle.

Creating the appearance that you are bigger than you really are has been the quest of the self-employed for decades. Computers and the Internet have made the task easier, but my recollection of how impressed I was with EWN's address reminds me of the power of perception.

While I've wanted to appear as a player among players, there is a fine line I have not been willing to cross. It's the deliberately false perceptions that some businesses project that offend me and other people as well. At the 1999 NSA Convention, Morley Safer and a crew from 60 Minutes spent a week following around Zig Ziglar, a member of the speakers association. They were getting footage for an upcoming segment on motivational speakers. All week, we saw Safer interviewing luminaries in the organization, the TV camera capturing every detail of the convention. When the show aired several months later, every member was notified and encouraged to tune in. That Sunday night, my husband Buddy and I sat down to watch the program. In a slow pan of the crowd I saw myself for a full second and a half attentively watching the speaker. I was tickled, and Buddy started punching my arm in excitement. I got a few phone calls from friends who had spotted me too. But the best response came in an e-mail from my colleague, Susan Keane Baker. She laughingly suggested that I rewrite my promotional materials to include the phrase, "as seen on 60 Minutes." Companies have done much more than that to publicize themselves.

CHAPTER 2

Systems

"Thinking of starting your own business? You'll need a business plan, a contact management system, $10,000 worth of office equipment, and employees or subcontractors. Good luck!"

"Uh, I think I'll just continue dabbling."

Somewhere between these two scenarios lies a third: learning what it takes to run an enterprise, lesson by lesson, year by year. It's true you'll need all of the above, but not now, not all at once. There's a lot of on-the-job training when you own your own company. It's like getting your MBA from the school of hard knocks.

LESSON 10

Getting advice from an expert is critical.
You'll save time and money.

Even back in the early '70s, when everything seemed so much simpler, purchasing machinery was a major event. My husband Buddy and I took some of our wedding money to Bloomingdale's to invest in a handheld calculator, an innovative piece of equipment that had recently come on the market. You have to put this in perspective. Pocket calculators costing $3.99 were not yet hanging off the racks at Staples. Staples didn't exist. Only department stores sold such equipment. We invested $80 in a Texas Instruments model—a significant amount of money in 1972. Similarly, in the 1980s when fax machines became popular, we went again as a couple—this time to Staples—to decide what size, design, and function we needed, and which machine we wanted to buy.

Before making a major tech purchase, I consult somebody for information, confirmation, or expertise. Ads and literature confuse me. I need to hear from a specialist exactly what I'm buying and how it will serve me. Then I make my decision. All my choices have made my business more efficient and competitive.

My friend Rick Wetzel is one such authority. As a developer for Apple Computer, he walked me through the purchase of my first Macintosh computer. We talked about the size of the monitor, the design of the keyboard, plus the printer and cables. Two weeks later, when it all got delivered, assembled, and plugged in, I called Rick in a panic. "Nothing's happening," I wailed. Calmly Rick looked at the invoice to see if everything we ordered was on there. It turned out that a teensy-weensy detail had been overlooked. We had forgotten to order the hard drive. Who knew?

Seven computer purchases later—I'm now on my second laptop—I still seek consultation on the latest and greatest machinery. From Palm Pilots to cell phones, there is too much information for one entrepreneur to comprehend. I prefer using experts to help me weed through gigabytes, analog versus digital, and roaming versus long distance. I want to spend my precious time doing what I do best—decorating eggs, writing, and talking about entrepreneurship.

I have found these experts through networking and meeting a variety of people in my associations. Most of the time these acquaintances and friends will provide the advice I need at no cost. It's one of the perks of being in a network—sharing expertise. My colleagues' generous spirits and wealth of information are the most reliable sources I have found.

LESSON 11

The clarity and direction gained from writing a business plan will give you a solid foundation for your business.

"Closed for Inventory" read the sign in a shop window as I walked down Madison Avenue one late July afternoon. I knew what that meant. Inside, the employees and owners were counting every piece of merchandise still on the shelves in order to verify their bookkeeper's figures. Past inventory minus what had been sold should equal current inventory. This is a boring, lengthy, and seemingly unrewarding job. Yet, when finished, the owners would know exactly where they stood.

I was in business for over ten years before I had to do a standard plan as homework for a course I was taking. I, like that shop on Madison Avenue, had to shut down my operations for a day or two and go through this lengthy, sometimes boring process, not knowing what the outcome would be. Like the store inventory, this exercise showed me exactly where I stood in my business. Although writing a business plan is pretty much a matter of filling in the blanks of a formula, it is not easy. Many of the empty spaces require a great deal of thought. I gained new insights and came to some new conclusions as I went through the process.

First I had to write a description of my business. I used to stammer in response to the question, "What do you do?" As simple and straightforward as that question was, it required massive thought to say succinctly how I spent the major part of my working day. After I had finished the marketing plan, I found I could lucidly tell anyone who asked that I was a designer of handcrafted art objects and jewelry pieces, selling to wholesale and retail markets, and licensing my designs to companies for use in other products.

Creating a goal or mission statement also took time. What sentence would inspire me when I lost my way, drive me to loftier goals, and keep me true to myself as an entrepreneur and human being? I decided that I wanted to be an internationally known and respected designer of handcrafted and licensed home decor.

Evaluating my market and competitors helped me establish guidelines for reaching my customers. Although my art form is distinctive, I had been exhibiting amid one hundred or more other artists who also produced unique treasures. While some shoppers were there solely to buy a pair of my earrings, most people came to craft shows looking for something "special." I realized I needed to create venues where everyone came to see me. Sales held in my studio proved to be a lucrative and rewarding alternative.

Listing staff is another part of the business plan. I hadn't really regarded the high school girls who worked in my studio after school as staff. That sounded so...formal. But they were on my payroll and had to be considered staff. Another new perception. Another notch on my entrepreneurial belt.

Describing my operations and production was straightforward. I listed the computer and printer, the copier and fax machine, plus all of the tools and machinery I'd acquired specifically for my craft. The whole list took up nearly two pages. "Hmmmm," I thought, "this is pretty impressive stuff."

One of the most valuable results of drafting the business plan came from the section on marketing. I knew that I needed frequent stimulation to continually generate fresh ideas and enthusiasm for my products. I wanted to create an advisory board for my business. I could then bounce ideas off the members so that I could generate new ideas. I therefore formed a mastermind group (see Support), which has become one of the engines that has driven my business.

After I had finished doing the business plan, I felt as though I'd been put through a wringer. I didn't look any different after I was finished, but something inside had definitely changed. The process of self-examination, thought, and articulation had transformed me. I had taken inventory and knew my stock cold.

LESSON 12

Never apologize for organizing your day.

A friend of mine had two daughters who attended a respected private school in Boston. Like many mothers, she took an active role in their education and became an involved parent. As her daughters grew, so did her interest in the school, and she eventually became a dean there. At a function in Boston, I was chatting with a group of women. One of them had children at my friend's school, so I asked her casually if she knew Nancy. She rolled her eyes and said, "Now there's a woman with an agenda." The implication was clear: Nancy was an opportunist, and anything she achieved was wrought not by hard work but by womanly contrivance. Having an agenda—a plan—was not looked upon kindly.

One spring weekend when another friend's daughter was getting married out of town, I shared a hotel room with two other women. We all woke up early the day of the wedding. I sat up in bed and said, "I have a plan. I'm going to do my meditation, and then go for a walk. I want to have breakfast at the waffle house up the block afterward. Anyone want to join me?" I didn't get any takers, but I followed my plan anyway and thought nothing about it again. Later that day, one of my roommates took me aside and informed me that I had annoyed her. I thought she was overreacting, but accepted her feelings and was glad she felt comfortable enough to voice them to me. Several months later, she brought it up again. "Remember how I told you that I didn't want to be told about your plan when we were in Baltimore? I realize now I was mostly annoyed because you had a plan…and I didn't."

Since I learned the tools and strategies for goal setting, I've had a plan for each day, each month, and each year of my life, and I've stopped apologizing for it.

L E S S O N   1 3

Attention to details matters.

Describing how I selected eggs to decorate took several paragraphs in my first book. When I was explaining the differences between white eggs and brown eggs I paused. I knew that I had heard something about their nutritional value, but couldn't remember. I knew that I could craft a sentence that disguised my lack of knowledge: Some people think that brown eggs have greater nutritional value. Or brown eggs are often perceived to have greater nutritional value.

But sentence number one made me feel like a fraud, and sentence number two bored me. I became curious and wanted to find out the truth. Students had asked me the question before, but it wasn't a detail that concerned me. My thoughts turned to Anne Lamott. *Bird by Bird: Some Instructions on Writing and Life* is one of my all-time favorite books. Reading it made me want to be a better writer. I used to resent interrupting my writing to research a word or a thought, but Anne Lamott considered it an adventure. For example, when she needed to find the exact word for that wire thing on top of a champagne cork she called the Christian Brothers Winery. This is how she described the process: "I got a busy signal. I really did. So I sat there staring off into space. I watched the movie in my mind of the many times I'd passed those vineyards and remembered how, especially in the early fall, a vineyard is about as voluptuous a place as you can find on earth." She made the process interesting, and the research became a journey. The word for that wire thing, she eventually learned, is hood.

I loved how Anne Lamott respected and crafted each word. She gave time and energy to do the job. Attention to detail in decorating eggs was my job. Why not transfer that ability and dedication to whatever I was focusing on? I called the University of Connecticut—well known for its agriculture department. A professor told me that the nutritional value is the same. I can now inform my students and my readers that there is no difference.

You don't hurt anyone's feelings
when you toss bulk mail.

My friend Carol was desperate and sent out an SOS. She was suffering from an inability to throw things out. When I arrived on the scene, her dining room table was covered from end to end (and about three inches deep) with mail, mostly unopened. I announced that our goal was to process everything that day. I chose the "rapid gross sort" for Carol, placing each item in one of four categories: toss, act, read, or file. As we approached each piece with these instructions, items that had to be tossed were easy. You didn't have to do anything after you tossed them in the wastebasket. The act file was a little harder. We made a tickler file, arranged by the date she had to pay bills or answer correspondence. Items to be read were divided into catalogs, magazines, and brochures. Each had a different folder. The "file" pile became the basis of her to-do list and remained manageable because the pile was not that big.

My friend really did not become as ruthless as I am. I'm at the point where I barely look at anything without a first-class stamp. If it's bulk mail I don't want to spend my time looking at it. Carol had too much sympathy for direct marketers. For instance, she had received a sample America Online disk and wanted to keep it. I asked her if she was unhappy with her current Internet provider. She confessed she wasn't actually on-line yet. In fact, she was still deciding what kind of a computer to buy. I assured her that she would be receiving demo disks or CDs weekly and that she could let go of this particular one.

She was still in a place I had once occupied—the "maybe someday" place that is nonproductive and keeps us stuck, overwhelmed with stacks of paper. No one enjoys sitting at a cluttered desk. When space is cleared, creative juices have room to flow. Carol's energy and enthusiasm mounted as her dining room table became increasingly more visible. Like me, she felt the psychological weight of all that unopened mail lifting off of her shoulders.

Dealing promptly and efficiently with incoming mail each day is a challenge for every entrepreneur. Sometimes calling a friend in to help tame the paper tiger is the best way to get out from under.

LESSON 1 5

Organizing yourself helps you
get to the questions that need answers.

You know the women (I'm convinced that men don't do this) who clean their houses before the cleaning lady comes? I took a page out of their book when I made an appointment to work with a professional organizer. We can take the people we mentor only as far as we have gone ourselves. The afternoon I spent at Carol's, helping her clear her cluttered table motivated me to do my own office cleaning. I already knew how to sort my mail and files. I needed to create new systems and called on a pro so that I could get to the next level.

I had several logjams I couldn't figure out. How do I keep all those wires on my desk—from my phone, my caller ID box, and my headset—under control? Where do I put my business card contacts that are multiplying daily? How do I organize the various components of my promotional kits—publicity, testimonial letters, and marketing pieces— so they remain within arm's reach without overwhelming me?

I began the job a week before the professional organizer was to show up. I wanted to make the best use of her time so I plowed through my entire office, drawer by drawer, cabinet by cabinet, so that I could produce a detailed list we would study together. This initial job worked wonders. It helped me formulate the questions I needed to ask. In addition, by going through all of my files I got rid of years' worth of unnecessary old paper. I discarded software and accompanying literature for a computer we had given to charity three years and one platform ago. I noticed multiple spiral-bound notebooks cluttering my desk. They contained computer questions and answers, daily records of my income and expenses, a gratitude list I'd been keeping for months. Could I eliminate or combine any of these?

My professional organizer streamlined all of my operations in a few well-spent hours. She suggested a five-section notebook for the contents of the several smaller ones. I purchased a stand that raised my phone to a new height and gave me a place below to store its accessories. A literature bin with twelve slots could hold my promotional materials and my data entry additions within easy reach. Best of all, I now have a clear head. I no longer have the physical clutter that used to cloud my thinking and hamper my activity. Not having those little scraps, wires, and distractions allows me to focus more clearly.

After she had completed her magic, I realized what really inspires me. It's not a trip to the museum, although that often works. It's not hearing a motivational speech, even though those help me reframe old thoughts and ideas. What really, really gets me inspired is a clean desk.

All the time, effort, and expense required to build systems for creating and maintaining a clean desk are worth it. Bringing in a professional has become an annual ritual for me, and I still organize as best I can before she comes.

LESSON 16

When someone gives you a lead, do the necessary work, even though the rewards aren't known in advance.

Somewhere between curtailing my full-time egg-decorating business and receiving the contract to write my first book, I entertained the notion that I would like to become the next Laura Ashley. I put out the word to my colleagues and began introducing myself as a textile designer at networking events.

Qualified leads come in unusual packages. At one Entrepreneurial Woman's Network lunch, a fellow artist tapped me on the shoulder and signaled me to come over to where she was sitting. She told me, "I was at my parents' house in Sag Harbor over Thanksgiving and was talking to their neighbor who is an interior designer. When I told him about your work, he said he would like to meet you." Sag Harbor sounded like the boonies to me, but being a polite woman, I kept listening. I didn't know Sag Harbor was an upscale artistic community on the tip of Long Island—a favorite getaway for successful New Yorkers.

Today I would qualify that lead by checking Google.com or Ask Jeeves on the Internet, but this was several years before that technology existed. So I had to trust the relationship and begin the pursuit of her parents' neighbor. Although it was a warm lead, the designer did not immediately respond to my call. I usually try once, leave a message, wait a week, and try again. Additionally, I might send a postcard or note letting them know that I'm trying to reach them. Then, I follow that with a third phone call a week or two later. If six varied attempts produce no response, I may go back to the person who gave me the lead, but I rarely pursue a lead more than six times.

We ultimately connected and arranged to meet at a restaurant he suggested in midtown Manhattan. I was sitting at the bar when the owner of the restaurant approached me. I told him I was waiting for Charles Morris Mount. It turned out that he had designed this restaurant's magnificent interior. "Can I get you anything while you're waiting?" the owner asked. It seemed as if doors were opening already. I was grateful I hadn't given up after the second or third unreturned call. I prayed he would like my portfolio.

Charles Morris Mount arrived at the appointed hour and was gracious in assessing my work. He listened to my career development and my new goals in the field of textile design. He liked my work enough to give me a referral to a design house in lower Manhattan that he used frequently. Their specialty was fabrics for institutions such as restaurants and hospitals.

I followed that lead to the president of the company. Again it took several attempts to connect, but the designer's name became the magic wand that got me a return call. The president passed me along to the head of design (more calls, more time) who booked an appointment with me. I brought in my portfolio for her assessment. Upon seeing my work she understood how she could apply my talents, although there was still one more person to see—the woman who would ultimately provide me with assignments and specifications.

Following this lead took a lot of time, phone calls, and perseverance, but thousands of dollars of work would result from that tap on the shoulder at a networking lunch.

L E S S O N   1 7

Get comfortable asking about money.

Polite young men and women are not brought up to say, "Show me the money!" Learning to ask how much you're going to be paid or informing a prospect about your fee are grown-up steps on the way to becoming a successful entrepreneur. For me, asking for my fee has been an ongoing struggle that has become easier only with practice and success.

After months of pursuing a lead to provide textile-painting services, I finally met the woman at the design studio who would be using my services. I thought I was home free. She started me off with a paint-by-numbers assignment that she offered me $25 per hour to do. I love it when there's clarity, even if it's less money than I wanted. Telling me the rate of pay saved me the discomfort of potential rejection and pain. The painting went well and the assignments continued.

After a few months of working with this arrangement, my client offered me a design assignment that allowed more creativity. I gladly accepted it. As I progressed with this freelance project, I began mentally calculating my time at the $25 per hour rate. However, this time I was not just painting the design, I was also conceiving and adapting it to required specifications. I estimated that the job would cost her $600 at the established rate. But I was feeling disgruntled, underpaid. This work required a higher level of skills than simply matching colors and filling them into an existing pattern. She was pleased with my finished work, but I had not yet negotiated a new fee. I knew I had nothing to lose by asking the question when the subject of invoicing came up, "Shall I bill this project the same way as the others you've given me?" Notice that nowhere in that question is a request for higher compensation. For me, it was still a step forward. "No," she replied. "We pay $1,200 to $1,500 per design. What do you think it's worth?" Given the choice, I opted for the high end and received it.

Slowly, I have added the money question or statement to every business relationship I've entered. I simply say, "Can we discuss the financial arrangements?" or "What does your budget allow for breakout sessions?" or "My fee is…"Sometimes the conversation that follows is pleasant. Sometimes it's difficult. But the best part is when it's over I know exactly where I stand and so does the client. I don't suffer the agony of not knowing. My sense of self-worth is reinforced by knowing ahead of time what rate I will get for the level of work I am doing. I don't have to work the question into a future conversation.

LESSON 18

Break down the items on your
to-do list into manageable pieces.

I've applied the principle "chunking it down" to my business on a regular basis. As soon as I write a goal down, like "organize an independent exhibition of my work," I can feel my heart start to race in fear and anticipation. My gremlins start saying things like, "Yeah, but how are you going to get people to come?" and "How will you produce enough inventory to fill a room?"

My therapist introduced me to the phrase "chunking it down." She said that although she thoroughly enjoyed entertaining friends, she would feel overwhelmed at the prospect of making a meal for fifteen people. So she learned how to chunk it down. She would break the work of a dinner party up into its multiple tasks (chunks) and then begin one of the chunks. The party became manageable when all she had to do at any given point in time was chop carrots for a salad.

The first thing I do when I'm thinking of doing something difficult is to show all the tasks on a road map that will take me there. Then I can convert this map into a list of things to do that gets plugged into my daily schedule.

When a friend and I worked together to create an independent exhibit of my work and hers, we mind-mapped together, creating categories such as locating a venue, getting PR, designing an invitation, finding a mail house, and hiring workers to assist at the event. Each of these categories had subcategories like finding a graphic artist to design the invitation and researching where to send our press releases.

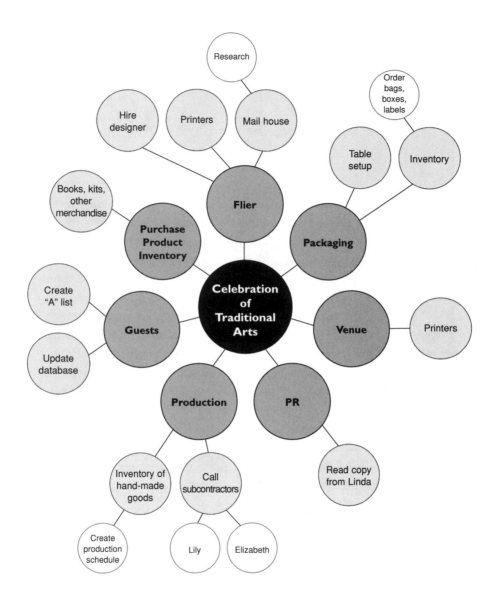

Mind Map

One category, producing the work we would sell (inventory), required different activities for each of us. My partner needed to search for vintage quilts to resell. I needed to make hundreds of pieces of art to sell. First I made a list of everything I wanted to produce for the show—decorated eggs, holiday ornaments, pins, earrings, and cufflinks made from eggshells. Then, I took a calendar and looked at how many days I had to prepare. I blocked out any day when I had commitments that would rule out studio time. Then I began plugging my production list into the available days. I found time on the calendar to craft each piece. I assigned the making of a log cabin-patterned egg to Tuesday. I would also have time that day to outline four egg ornaments. On Wednesday I planned to make four Ukrainian deer pins and two pairs of matching earrings. And so I went, chunking down my list into manageable daily activities. Once I had assigned the entire list to specific days I took a look at my filled calendar and felt a sense of relief. It was doable. And there was plenty of time to spare.

A frequently asked question at many of my exhibits has been "How do you find the time?" We all have the same 24 hours per day. The most important aspect of chunking it down is that when the task shows up on your calendar, you do it then without procrastination. It's the cumulative effect of putting tasks off that make them seem insurmountable. Chunking them down is a success formula not only for socializing but also for business events and lifelong achievement.

L E S S O N   1 9

It's your business, and you are in charge of every aspect of it, even the jobs you delegate.

Brian Tracy, creator of *The Psychology of Achievement,* has a mantra: "I am responsible." It was one of my least favorite things to hear on his tapes. In fact, I hated the sound of those words. They took away all my excuses, self-pity, self-righteousness, and my favorite face-saving device, blaming others. Of course, I also knew that he was dead right, which is why I particularly hated it. For example, following a wildly successful craft show, I was calculating all my sales, including the charge receipts, when I noticed that several charges had not been through the credit card swipe machine. This meant that these sales would be invalid, because I didn't have a record of the customers' card numbers. I realized these receipts had been processed by the assistant I had hired to help me at the show and was furious because it represented hundreds of dollars in lost sales.

My first response normally would have been to call this woman and vent my anger and frustration. Then I began to consider Brian's mantra. How could I possibly be responsible for her obvious blunder? The answer came slowly—I had not taken sufficient time to review the processing of credit cards with her, I had not watched her handle some of the sales, I had not had the foresight to create a simple instruction sheet for her so that the swiping would be an idiot-proof task. I was indeed responsible.

Jane Fonda's words, "no pain, no gain," do work. But why is it that the only way I learn these lessons is when they cost me money?

L E S S O N 2 0

Writing down your goals is the beginning of the transformation process.

"I'm going to be an author when I grow up because I love books. I want to go to Mount Holyoke College. I'm going to marry a millionaire and have a mink coat and lots of jewels. When I get married I'm going to have two children."

Written in the hand of an eight-year-old, this crayon-illustrated essay on lined paper hangs in my friend Aimee's loft in Manhattan. She lives there with her millionaire husband, Joe, and two daughters, Louisa and Emma. She has written a 300-page novel and is working on a second. Aimee and I have been friends since 1967, when we met in an introductory theater arts course in college. I've taken two courses in goal setting, but never was the power of the written goal evidenced more clearly than with Aimee's framed commitment from thirty-plus years ago—before most people were even talking about goal setting.

When Laura, my youngest child, was three years old, I signed up for a weekend workshop on goal setting. It was a luxurious opportunity to delve into my heart's desires. I had two days to be introspective, to dream big dreams, and to understand the principles of laying out goals for myself. I had begun listening to audiotapes that motivated me to take a closer look at my life. *Choosing Your Own Greatness* by Wayne Dyer and *How to Make Your Life an Adventure* by Roger Dawson are two that had a major impact on my outlook and attitude.

One of the exercises we had to do at that workshop was to set a long-term goal. It was a chance to take a good long look ahead, to consider what we'd like to be doing in a year, three years, ten or more years. Since my three children were all under ten at the time, I had not yet looked past PTA meetings and volunteerism. What the heck, I thought, why not create a wish list. What's the harm? I wrote down that in ten to fifteen years I wanted to be a motivational speaker. I wanted to change people's lives the way Wayne Dyer and Roger Dawson had changed mine. I had no area of expertise to speak about. I had no message and I had no audience in mind. Still, I wrote down that goal.

The instructors at the workshop taught me that something physiological happens when the eye sees the hand writing a message. Writing "I want to be a professional speaker" and then seeing the words on paper gave me an immediate rush of adrenaline, and my heart started to beat faster.

I made the decision to take my business to a new level. I put in more hours working on my egg decorating, trying new designs, gaining expertise in my craft. Several years later when my youngest child was nine and we had put away most of the toys, my husband and I converted our family room into a quasi-home office. We shared the space, a computer, and a copier. To become more successful, I needed to become more productive. To become more productive, I was going to need a more efficiently designed space. I set the goal to convert our newly created home office into a studio for my business.

No sooner had I committed the goal to paper than I attended a luncheon for my Entrepreneurial Woman's Network and found myself seated next to an architectural designer who had her portfolio with her. I was able to look at it, and what at first appeared to be an overwhelming project—remodeling the family room—became manageable with her expertise. My renovated studio was completed in less than seven months.

The new space changed more than my productivity. It enhanced my self-image. Now I felt I could invite customers over, hold studio sales, and enjoy being photographed in my new space. Sales and income increased, and I began to realize that I was achieving at a higher level as a result of remodeling my space.

Incrementally I was taking the steps necessary to become a motivational speaker. I was developing expertise in entrepreneurship so that other people would be interested to hear how I did it. It would be true to say that I wrote down long-term goals and achieved them. But the transformation was slow, step by step, inch by inch. Writing my goals down began the process.

L E S S O N   2 1

Whenever you receive a compliment,
simply say, "Thank you."

Gracious acknowledgment of a compliment, in business or in your personal life, shows that you respect the giver and that you realize you're worthy of such praise. When my youngest child was in third grade, she agreed to go on her first overnight field trip. I envisioned a teary farewell the morning of the expedition. We got a call before we were about to leave, asking if we'd pick up a classmate of Laura's en route. I asked my daughter's permission, thinking that she might have wanted the emotional moment of departure to be more private, but she was okay with it.

On the way to Caitlin's I said, "It was very sweet of you to include Caitlin this morning." Laura answered, "It fills me with joy to have her." I was so moved by her magnanimous spirit I practically shouted, "Laura, you are joy!" She recoiled in her seat and said, "Oooooooohhh, Mom, please." I immediately went into a lecture mode. I wanted her to understand and value praise—a lesson I had learned the hard way. I told her that story. One day, when I was at a show exhibiting my work, a customer came to my booth and admired the sweater I was wearing. I looked down at what I was wearing, tugged at the garment with my thumbs and forefinger, and said, "Loehmann's," a premium designer discount chain. She was crestfallen. I had diminished her words by rejecting the compliment.

"So," I told Laura, "from that moment forward, I changed my behavior. Whenever I receive a compliment, I take a deep breath, sometimes I even put my hands over my heart—taking in the words—and say thank you. Do you want to try that again, Laura? She nodded. I repeated, "Laura, you are a joy," and she nodded as a way of thanking me. She looked down at her jacket, fingered the lapel, coyly looked up at me with a twinkle in her eye and said, "Loehmann's."

LESSON 22

Before you hire people to provide special services,
get a recommendation from a person
who is familiar with their abilities.

When I needed a dentist, I asked my friend Betsy for the name of hers. I knew it was a safe bet because she was so thorough in whatever she tackled. I knew she would have done all the research. I was right. Her dentist became our family's painless and competent caregiver until he retired. I wish that there had been an egg-decorating Betsy in my business life—a vetted source I could go to for every referral I needed. Instead, I had to learn other methods for acquiring good help. I still haven't come up with a fail-safe solution.

A well-qualified, word-of-mouth referral is my preferred method for hiring any service provider. Seeking out sources used by successful friends and colleagues is the surest route to happy business relationships. Placing ads or getting secondhand referrals is a gamble. When I wanted a new design for my booth at craft shows, I had two experiences that were costly and not satisfactory. I tried the referral method, but didn't know the source well enough to trust his reliability. I asked a professor at a highly regarded professional school in New York City for the name of a student designer, and he told me about a woman—a student of his—who lived outside Manhattan.

She prepared a magnificent design that would use elegant yet inexpensive materials. Her design estimate was within my budget, and we made an agreement to work together. I was feeling proud of myself and cocky that my method of seeking out a new designer was working so well. However, though this young woman was a creative genius, it turned out she was a nut case. After I had given her my deposit, her behavior verged on insanity. During the course of constructing the display, she became visibly pregnant and claimed immaculate conception. Throughout our months working together she continued to express bewilderment about her condition and how it came to be. My calls inquiring about her work on my design went unanswered. As my deadline approached, I began to panic. I had seen nothing yet. I ended up driving to her home, hours away, to monitor the progress. In the end, I used the display only one time because it was too bulky to transport and too difficult to erect by myself.

The next designer I hired came up with a more functional display, but his follow-through was sloppy and disappointing. I had to hold back some of his payment and confront him in order to get the display up to the quality we had agreed upon—it was a very unpleasant experience. That referral had been second or third hand from someone who worked in the same building that housed his studio.

I prefer to talk about my successful hires because they are much less painful. For years Mary Quinlan, the chair of the Norwalk High School art department, has recommended one phenomenal art student after another. She understands the nature of the work I do and the delicate hands required to assist me. As her good students reach their senior year, she starts looking over her juniors so she can keep me in production when my current worker graduates.

When Liz Wheeler, one of Mary's recommendations, was about to go off to college, I teased her by asking if she by any chance had a sister to take her place. She did. Rachel Wheeler was a sophomore at the time and worked in my studio for two years after Liz left. She was not only a terrific artist and helper, but also a brilliant English student who proofread my first book.

One of my best employees, Elizabeth Bullis-Wiese, recommended herself to me. A friend of mine had referred Elizabeth to do landscape work outside our house. While working in the yard, Elizabeth asked to peek in my studio to see what kind of work I did. As a part-time artist herself, she was intrigued and offered her services to me as an assistant. During her off-season, Elizabeth has done production work for me for several years.

Having an employee in my studio benefits me on many levels. First, my workload is less, and delegating tasks frees me to do what I do best. Secondly, working at home alone can be extremely isolating. I lose my sense of reality and perspective. Having another person present with whom to discuss new ideas helps a lot. Getting a second opinion is invaluable, and having that capability at my disposal several hours a week is a necessary component of my success.

I've learned in my twenty-plus years in business that the best way to find help is through known connections—people in either my classes or networks who understand the nature of my business. Second to a vetted referral is being excruciatingly careful in detailing the task at hand so that I and the person I am hiring are both clear on my expectations and how they will be carried out.

LESSON 23

Be open to new encounters.
Be careful not to prejudge people.

I believe in serendipity. My preferred hotel had been fully booked so I ended up at another hotel. The next morning I found a table in the dining area where I could quietly read my book and relax over coffee before the day's event. The breakfast crowd that morning was large, so I wasn't surprised when a woman asked me if she could sit down at my table. I made a conscious decision to put down my book and find out why the universe had placed this particular individual in my space. She was older than me, exotically coiffed, and bedecked with strands of beads.

"What brings you to Massachusetts?" I asked. "I'm here for my granddaughter's middle-school graduation," she replied. I was hoping for something more interesting.

"And what brings you here?" she graciously added. Ahhhh. At least it wouldn't be all about her. It's important to note two things here. Only two sentences into the conversation and already the judgments were flooding my brain. I'd invalidated this woman's role on earth after one sentence and then readmitted her because she'd shown interest in me. "I'm here for a meeting of the National Speakers Association. I'm a professional speaker," I replied.

"Oh, what do you speak about?" She was becoming more interesting by the minute. "I'm an artist. I talk about turning your passion into a business."

"I'm an artist, too," she said. Hat of judgment back on my head. "Really?" Many people think they're artists. I decided to start with the all-important question that divides the amateurs from the pros. "Do you sell your work?"

"Yes, I do." "Oh, really. Where?" Still trying to find out if she was for real or a "wannabe." "New York," she said. Buffalo, I thought. Anyone can sell art in Buffalo.

"Manhattan," she clarified. "Fifty-seventh Street." I reframed the situation. While my first instinct was to help a naive aspirant to the arts, the tables were now turned and I was in a position to benefit from a New York artist's experience.

"What kind of work do you do?" I am not very current on the New York art scene, but I hoped to show a modicum of intelligence about her field. "I paint very large canvasses with autobiographical materials, then add stitches to the canvasses."

Even though my knowledge of contemporary artists is slim, the minute she said "stitches," a bell went off in my head. "May I ask your name?" "Faith Ringgold." "OMIGOD!" The one contemporary artist whom I really admire and whose work I have seen dozens of times in *The Crafts Report* and *FiberArts*—two trade magazines for people in the arts—is Faith Ringgold.

"Would you mind waiting here for a minute? I would love to show you what I do." I ran to the car where I had packed my first book and my decorated eggs. I brought them in and placed them before her like an offering at the altar. Faith proceeded to leaf through my book page by page, commenting, smiling, and appreciating my work.

Then I opened up the box of eggs so that she could see the real things. I carry them in a cardboard egg carton, just the way you would pick them up in a supermarket. I always enjoy watching people's reaction when they see these miniature works.

Although her eyes and her smile delighted me, it was the question that followed that would remain with me." How much are they a dozen?" No one had ever asked me that question. When I began the craft over twenty-five years ago, my eggs sold for eight dollars apiece. With experience, great press, and increased self-esteem, the price had escalated to $250 per egg. The calculator in my head rapidly multiplied that amount times twelve. "Three thousand dollars," I replied. She said, "If I were you, I would only offer them by the dozen, and I would sell them in a glass egg carton." Brilliant! A million-dollar idea.

Had I stayed at the first hotel and had I chosen to read my book and not deigned to go outside of my comfort zone to initiate a conversation with a total stranger, I would have missed what turned out to be one of the most exciting and profitable encounters in my career. The more open I stay to what the universe plants in my path, the more spectacular the journey.

CHAPTER 3

Not Every Day Is A Winner

I had a large order due. My son was home from school sick and
had to be taken to the pediatrician. The high school girl who
works for me had to make up an exam and couldn't come. A
severe snowstorm was predicted on the radio, and I had made
plans to meet a friend for lunch the next day. It was a rare treat I
had carefully planned. No tragedy, but did it all have to happen at
the same time? I always thought that if you showed up and did
what you were supposed to do, everything would be nice. And a
lot of times, it is. But dealing with the days that are not nice takes
patience. For me, rolling with the punches is learned behavior. I
still yearn for days that aren't hard.

LESSON 24

There are always days that are slated for growth or learning. Stay with them and don't get upset.

Pedro Boregaard, a jeweler I know, described a situation I am familiar with. He had worked on a pin for days, and the more he worked on it, the more he knew it wasn't the way he wanted it. He completed the brooch, but knew that it still wasn't right. He moved on. The next dozen or so pieces were effortless and perfect. I find if I stay with a difficult process, there is a lesson to be learned.

For example, a woman commissioned me to make an egg celebrating the iron gates at Brown University that were opened only two times a year, at convocation and graduation. She wanted it as a gift for her daughter who was graduating from Brown.

I had to paint that majestic image on an eggshell. I worked out a design, dyed the egg, and proceeded to lay it out. Halfway through the process, I was fairly certain that the black dye was not dark enough. But I continued anyway because I wanted to see if I could get away with it and if the rest of the design would work. When I completed the egg and removed the wax to reveal the colors beneath, my heart sank a little. It was just okay. It wasn't great. The gates were closer to gray than black and didn't seem to convey enough power. A friend who taught art stopped by the next day, and I asked his opinion, hoping since he didn't know what I was striving for, the egg would still appeal to him. I really didn't want to do it over again. His words were nonjudgmental, but final, "My eye wants to see more contrast."

I started over, making sure this time the bath of black dye had totally saturated the egg before I proceeded. The egg was perfect—I had achieved my original goal. The customer called me as soon as it arrived to thank me profusely.

I'm always looking for the shortcut, but sometimes there isn't one. It's always best to push for the correct solution.

I saw this poem recently that describes the process perfectly.

It is a pleasure
When, after a hundred days
Of twisting my words
Without success suddenly
A poem turns out nicely

It is a pleasure
When spreading out some paper
I take a brush in hand
And write far more skillfully
Than I could have expected.

Haiku by Tachibana Akemi (1812–1868)
Translated by Donald Keene

L E S S O N   2 5

Contact your customers frequently,
but don't worry if they don't respond quickly.

When I think about sending out yet another mailing, (I'm talking three to four per year), I wonder if it's worth the effort. So I go over what I do when I receive a catalog. For example, when I get L.L.Bean's catalog, I'll see something I like, but think I'll wait until the next time when they send me another catalog. However, when I experienced the same attitude in my own customers, I wasn't happy. I remembered them coming to my booth at a craft show and admiring my work, but they were having trouble making a decision. They would leave, saying, "I can't decide. I'll see you in the Spring." Of course I wanted them to buy right then and there.

It reminded me of my mother's advice about boys, "Don't be so available." (Slightly different from "If the milk is free, why buy the cow?") But I knew what she meant. I wanted to be perceived as hard to get so I stopped doing shows, and I finally came to the conclusion that I had to send out frequent mailings without worrying about responses. Often a customer will call me with an order, saying she was thinking of me just before she received my catalog. This sort of thing, a personal phone call along with an order, happens a lot. The remarkable thing is that it works with different people each time, creating a revolving list of customers, exactly what I want. I don't want to pester my really good customers to death. So if someone is paying attention to me for the first time in four years, that's okay.

L E S S O N   2 6

It's important to know when to discard something you already have for the promise of something better to come.

I was running a successful business out of my makeshift studio in our converted family room. Orders were coming in; I was decorating eggs at a decent pace, it was all working well. But I kept tripping over the wires that connected the new computer and printer. The telephone was located on the opposite side of the room from the computer. The file cabinets jutted out of the wall, blocking the path from my design area to my egg decorating area. Every time I made a mental note that these small inconveniences should be improved, I didn't want to make the effort.

However, once I realized that a renovated studio would make an enormous difference in my production and in my self-image, I moved forward and found an architectural designer to map out all the areas I envisioned. Just imagining a dedicated area for dealing with epoxy and another area to be used solely for shipping lightened my heart. Not only would I be more efficient, but also my spirit would be uplifted. My creativity, enthusiasm, and productivity would increase.

What I didn't anticipate was the sheer drudgery of getting through the renovation. "What was I thinking?" I asked my husband as we watched the movers packing up every piece of equipment and furniture in my studio and carrying it into our living room where I was going to set up shop in the interim—hopefully only for thirty days.

I was miserable. The light in the living room was dreadful. Interruptions were constant. Our kids used the room to watch TV, talk on the phone, and relax. Close quarters without a private sanctuary made relations between me and my family strained.

It's always darkest before the dawn. Just when I thought I couldn't stand it a moment longer, the renovation was completed and I began moving my equipment back into my studio and out of the family's space. A week later the room was painted, the floor tiles were laid, and I had a magnificent space to work. The raw emotions of the month before were transformed from anger to deeper intimacy. We had survived the renovation.

Going into the hell of remodeling, I knew I would be rewarded if I could just be patient and persevere. By resisting the temptation to settle for satisfactory short-term rewards, I ended up with greater long-term benefits. I am convinced that entrepreneurs can measure their success by their willingness to forgo immediate results for the promise of greater, more lasting gains.

LESSON 27

Consider yourself lucky if there are only minor irritations in your day.

It takes a lot to move me out of my studio space. I hate leaving it to run errands. I would like to hire someone to do them for me, but there never are enough errands to justify it.

After focusing closely on a project for a few hours, I usually take a break mid-morning and do the errands together with my mail run. One day I decided to start out early in order to wrap up some annoying minor tasks—banking, a pickup at the printers two towns away, and a purchase at the office supply store. The store and my printer would be open by 7:00 a.m., so I figured I would start with them and end up at the bank, where the drive-through window opens at 8:30 a.m.

Into the life of any entrepreneur a little rain must fall. Considering the possibilities, this catalog of a morning's events seems minor, but to the person involved it can be major, even overwhelming. Here's the scenario: I leave my house at 7:45 a.m., giving myself forty-five minutes to accomplish two tasks before I land at the bank window in time for the 8:30 a.m. opening.

I drive to my farthest destination first to pick up a job at the printer. I pull up at the building and know at once that the hand-lettered sign stuck with tape on the door is not a message I want to read. "Back in one hour." I have a system. I always keep a folder of magazine articles and newsletters in my car or in my bag that I can pull out anytime I find myself in a holding pattern. Doctor's offices, bank lines, and airports drive me crazy if I don't have something to do to pass the time. This particular morning I don't have my folder with me. To sit there stewing is not an option. I leave in a huff.

Next on my list is the office supply store where I need a special mailing label for a marketing piece I'm going to send out. (To make my mailings as personal as possible, I like to use transparent labels. They give the illusion that the address is printed right on the envelope.) The office supply store is out of the transparent labels. I am now two for two in the failure column.

Sometimes I begin to wallow in self-pity. "Why is this happening to me? I'm cursed. Poor me." With a glimmer of hope, I think, "At least I'll be first in line at the bank." I am pleased to see there's no line of cars, but when I drive up, I understood why. There's a note announcing the hydraulic function at the drive-through window is broken. And the bank won't open its doors until 9:00 a.m.

Inevitably, after moaning and groaning about the unfairness of life and my burdens, I will encounter someone far less fortunate than me— a person with a visible handicap that won't be better tomorrow. And I straighten up and stop crying. So every day now I take the time to list the things I am grateful for. It helps remind me how lucky I really am.

LESSON 28

Occasionally the planets may line up to force you to take time off.

"I can't reach any of my prospects on the phone, my assistant is away for a few days, and I'm waiting for one of my tools to be repaired. I don't seem to be getting anything done." " Sounds like the universe wants you to take a vacation," a friend said with a smile.

How much more information did I need? Toughing out those black periods by trying to accomplish something is often an exercise in frustration. I remember I woman I met at a networking luncheon who stood out because she was walking with a cane and had an impressive-looking bandage on her foot. I introduced myself and pointed to her injury. "It's nothing glamorous. I was walking down the driveway to pick up my mail and tripped on a pebble. I broke two bones in my foot. The funny thing is, for weeks before this happened I kept repeating to myself, 'I need a break. I need a break.'"

The more I learn how to read the "breaks" the universe sends me and respond to those breaks by taking time off, the less likely I'll wind up frustrated or walking with a cane.

LESSON 29

It's hell learning how to use
new gadgets and new systems,
but remember you are not alone.

I always wanted to be one of those sophisticated business types who use credit cards to make long distance calls. I'd see them rush out between seminars to the pay phones, no fishing in their pockets for quarters, no dealing with an operator—just dialing. I envied them and wanted to be like them.

Finding a provider for a telephone credit card was easy. A woman in my network gave me the name of a long-distance carrier that had good rates. I contacted them and was sent a calling card with instructions on how to use it. I was assigned a code and told I could dial anywhere in the world from a hotel room, pay phone, or friend's home. But first I had to learn how, and then I had to practice.

I never like the practice part. I don't want to go through the messy, uphill learning curve—I want instant know-how. I'm aware that I have to master new things at my own slow pace. I'm aware that the small, incremental steps eventually turn into competence. I know that, yet every time I have to become competent at something new, I balk at the unfairness of it all.

To register with the telephone card people, I had to dial 35 digits and wanted to scream when I got through. The very first time I had to use the card was at a retreat run by the Elderhostel people. (I was teaching them how to decorate eggs.) The only means of communication to the outside world at the retreat was a pay phone in the dining hall. I had to make several business calls, and thought, wow, what a great opportunity to try out my new service. I punched in thirty-five numbers to make that first call, my eyes glued to the instruction card. I made a second call and cursed the system for being so cumbersome.

Between calls I scoured the card for a way to make the process easier. When I made two calls in one trip to the telephone, I discovered that if I pressed the pound key at the end of the first call, I would get a dial tone and could simply punch in the next phone number without entering the other twenty-five numbers. As I continued using the phone during my stay there, I began to notice that it was getting easier—my fingers seemed to know where to move on the keys. By the end of my stay there, I could make a call without referring to the instruction card at all. I had memorized all the numbers and could execute them with great speed— just like those cool, sophisticated types.

The anguish in learning to use new gadgets and new systems is something nobody talks about, probably because we think we are the only stupid ones—that everyone else in the world can do it easily.

LESSON 30

In the long run you learn more from your failures than from your successes.

Self-pity fueled my existence. I used to enjoy complaining and appreciated the attention I received. Later when I began examining my motives more closely and noticed that my pool of sympathizers was thinning out, I became embarrassed by my behavior and decided to change. But I didn't grow up without first experiencing pain. We learn from our failures, not from our successes. This is humbling to realize. I wish that there were an easier way.

An experience at my first trade show helped me examine my values. I was exhibiting for the first time and had not taken any orders at all, whereas the woman next to me was wondering how she could handle the $7,000 worth of orders she had taken that day. And this was only the first day of the show. What irked me most was that she was exhibiting papier-mâché witches, pumpkins, and skeletons, stuff that might have been kitsch, but were they art? The show was subtitled "the finest in American handcraftsmanship." I wondered how she had even been juried in.

At the end of the show, although I had adequate sales and a good-sized list of potential customers to add to my database, I wondered if it was the right market for me, but came to the conclusion that my intricate designs were not easy for people to see and judge. They might have to see them several times before they bought any of my eggs. I made the decision then that exhibiting at shows might not be the best venue for my work.

LESSON 31

Self pity will get you nowhere. You have to respond to a tough situation directly with action.

It's one thing to find yourself in a bad situation and try to improve it. It's another, to stand pat and do nothing.

Suffering through the humiliation of no sales is humbling, to say the least. One time I was at a show and was happy with my display. But once the crowds started filtering through the tents, I noticed that they would glance at the display, but not enter my booth. I could have moved my display farther forward, but I'll never know whether that solution would have worked because I made the decision not to care. Talk about self-pity; that was self-destruction.

Somewhere, way back when, I learned that there were lots of shoulds and should nots out there: If I work this hard and produce beautiful products, I should be able to sell them; if my work is prettier than another artist's, I should outsell them. But that isn't always so. That level of expectation always leads to disappointment. Now, when I analyze a situation and see that I could wallow in self-pity or improve it, I act promptly. The longer I wait, the more likely I am to stamp my feet at the unfairness of the world. If I want to move forward, I have to take the step right way. The longer I delay the action, the more likely I am to dive into the morass of self-pity. If I act rather than react, I am more likely to move forward. I'm also working on acquiring the grace to admire the people I know who take action rather than suffer.

L E S S O N   3 2

As you work, continually evaluate what is the next thing you have to do in order to succeed.

Particularly because I have a home office, I frequently have to take care of the daily trivia, along with my work. Sometimes I feel overwhelmed, and that's when I know it's time to evaluate the importance of any task. Here's an example. Time savers hold a special place in my heart. When I am introduced to a product that will save me precious minutes or even seconds, I consider it. The first time I saw a shampoo dispenser in a hotel bathroom, I thought, "What a great idea—no more taking the caps off and putting them on! " And then when I saw advertised in a catalog a dispenser for all the products I used in the shower, I realized it would give me even more time to enjoy the streaming hot water and less time fiddling with bottles and jars. I ordered it, feeling quite smug— I had discovered a better mousetrap.

That was short-lived. Within days, the dispenser became clogged and stopped working. I called customer service. "We'll be happy to refund your money on that product. But we've discontinued our relationship with the vendor and can't contact them. If you like, you can take it up with them directly." Well, I really liked the idea of the dispenser and had enjoyed using it. I made an attempt, got a recording, waited for a call back, and tried once more. When I saw the "call again" on my to-do list a week later I thought to myself, "How important is this right now? Not at all." I postponed the task. When that date arrived, I still didn't want to spend the time it would take to get the replacement dispenser or parts. So I crossed it off my list and let it go.

Now, let's translate this experience to work. One morning I talked about my work to a group of people. One of the men who attended was very enthusiastic about my eggs and wanted a special one painted to look like a Volkswagen. He ordered one and was absolutely delighted by it when I sent it to him. He thought that everyone in his VW club would love it. He thought it would make a great gift for VW dealers throughout the world—as an incentive for salespeople, gifts for key customers, and so on. I began to pursue that lead, but after several dead ends I asked myself, "How important is this right now? Where will it lead? Do I really want to make fifty or a hundred VW eggs? Is that a market I want to pursue?" My gut was my guide. I said, "Forget it."

LESSON 33

When someone asks you how you got that incredible break, the simple answer is hard work.

One afternoon a production crew that included a cameraman, sound guy, producer, and director plus two dot-comers spent six hours in my studio taping an interview for network television. That opportunity had the potential to result in the best exposure my small business had encountered so far. I was excited and told my walking partner about it the next day. When she asked me how it happened, in my mind I went through the many stages that led to it.

It all started this way. Nine years earlier during a routine checkup, the dental assistant and I chatted, and between rinses I described my work to her. She asked me if I'd seen *Victoria,* a relatively new magazine which had a monthly feature of unusual business cards from all over the country and suggested I send my card in. I trusted her instincts, and promptly went to the nearest shop to check it out. The magazine was gorgeous, and the page Julie described was just right for my kind of business. I mailed in my card.

Victoria checked me out thoroughly. They contacted me for more information to ensure that I could handle the surge of orders that would follow such publicity. I had to assure them that I had support materials showing my products and prices. I also had to be interviewed by an editor at the magazine. It worked. My card and one of my intricately decorated eggs were featured in the April issue.

In May I met the Editor-in-Chief at an American Women's Economic Development conference. She suggested that *Victoria* do a story on my work. More opportunities arose, including featuring my jewelry in their circular, participating in a chat room online with their readers, and speaking on a panel at a conference they sponsored.

Then *Victoria* chose seventy women including me to profile in a book, *The Business of Bliss—How To Profit From Doing What You Love*. This prompted the television company to contact me.

Here's the true answer to the question, how did it happen. I pursued a lead, followed up, showed up, stayed in touch, sought out future opportunities, pursued those, and continued this pattern for nine years.

I told my walking partner, "Just lucky, I guess."

L E S S O N   3 4

It's easy to save money by using your time,
or to save time by using your money
but it's hard to decide which.

At one time I was smug and thought I was saving money by handling
every aspect of a bulk mailing. I designed the flier on my computer,
printed it out, and made 300 copies. I folded, stapled, and added postage
to each copy. I attached the address labels that I'd printed out from my
database. It probably took me three hours to complete the task. I had
saved myself a whopping eighteen dollars. I could have used the time to
produce a piece of art that would sell for $300. On the other hand, I
spent a hundred dollars for an hour of computer tutoring when I could
have picked up the manual to figure it out for myself.

A friend's story drove home my own lunacy. When the post office
increased the price of stamps from 32 to 33 cents, my friend bought
some. However, he had thirteen pieces of mail with 32 cent stamps
already glued on. So he decided to go to the post office to buy thirteen
1 cent stamps. But when he saw the serpentine line, he placed 33 cent
stamps on the already stamped letters, put them in the mail chute, and
walked out. His biggest mistake was telling his wife. She was outraged
at the total waste of money. Tit for tat. He told her the next time she
went to the airport, she could just as easily use a shuttle rather than the
limousine service she always insisted on. She shut up.

LESSON 35

Tackle today's tasks today.
Don't postpone anything that you really have to do.

I was at a conference and saw a woman who had so much confidence, she stood out. I wanted to be her and I needed to know how she came to have it. I introduced myself, and started with the typical networking banter. Soon we went beyond the chitchat and talked about getting together for lunch. Karen asked the all-important question, "When?" I had noticed that Karen was holding an impressive attaché case. As she uttered the word "when," she unzipped its leather case, revealing a time management system the likes of which I'd never seen. It was more than twice the size of the impressive Filofax planners that people were carrying in the late 1980s—before Palm Pilots were in vogue. Instead of squeezing my name into one of those little squares on a calendar page, she penciled my name smack in the middle of a full-sized sheet of paper labeled March 20. I now occupied the 12:00–1:00 p.m. slot. An entire page devoted to one day!

Turned out that Karen was a franchise owner as well as a certified facilitator for Priority Management, a worldwide organization whose mission is to enhance productivity. After our lunch, I wanted more. I signed up for her workshop—a commitment requiring two half days of training. Karen followed up by visiting my home office to see how I was managing the implementation of the technology she'd introduced.

Before I learned Karen's method of addressing one day at a time, I used a calendar planner that allowed me to see all of my activities for the week at once. Because I had a strong need to check things off my list, I would find myself shifting my glance over to the next calendar day's activities before I tackled the more onerous tasks facing me today. I knew it was easier for me to reschedule the post office errand for tomorrow than it was to make the phone call asking for an order today. So I would often postpone tasks I didn't want to do.

With Karen's system, the next day was not visible. Therefore, I stayed in today and did all the things on my to-do list. I learned to take one day at a time. This slogan, taken from Alcoholics Anonymous has been a life-altering mindset for my approach to time management. Thank you, Karen Stanley.

L E S S O N   3 6

Make a commitment to improve yourself a little bit each day. You'll see the results.

Alan Weiss, author of Million Dollar Consulting, advocates a philosophy, the "1% Solution™," which challenges us to improve at a minimum rate of 1 percent a day. Weiss's "solution" has become a watchword for me. Thanks to him, I often tell myself, "You can do that better, 1% better." Sometimes this practice doesn't produce results immediately. At first it hardly shows. And I resent this—when I work harder, I want to see fireworks.

I noticed this pattern as I was preparing a mailing for a client. Instead of including some information about a web site she ought to look at, I attached a post-it telling her simply that she ought to check it out, and I sealed the package. Then I had this feeling in my gut, always a signal that I was not comfortable with what I had just done. I examined the feeling and heard the voice beneath it say, "She's your client. Why don't you look up the site yourself and send her the information? Save her that step. Make yourself a resource for her. Go the extra 1 percent." I opened up the package, did the research on the web site, and sent her the information. As insignificant as this sounds, to me it was major. Once I've put something on the pile to go to the post office, I'm done with it. It's almost heresy to change that pattern. This time I chose to do it right, to do it better.

Two things happened. I discovered more about that particular site, which became very valuable to my work, and I became the kind of person who takes that extra step. As with any muscle, once I flexed it, it became easier to work it. I'm sure my client had no idea of the process

I went through. She may or may not have benefited from the information I sent. But I benefited from my action by extending myself, by growing that 1 percent, and by becoming the kind of person who takes responsibility and initiative.

LESSON 37

Exert control over your own destiny.

My friend Cindy says that entrepreneurs experience only two emotions—high and low. I go to the post office every day. When I get there and open my post office box, I look through the contents anxiously. Here's a good day: nestled in a thick stack of third-class catalogs, mailers, and newsletters, there's a check and a handwritten letter from a person I really admire. (Orders rarely come through the mail these days. They are either faxed, or e-mailed, or come on the net. So I'm never disappointed when I find no orders in my box.) A really bad day is a totally empty box. But even worse is the day when I open the box and see something promising—a single handwritten envelope—and open it eagerly only to find it's a scrawled request from a customer asking to be deleted from my mailing list.

I used to exhibit at juried craft shows. Acceptance at a premier craft show is not easy. Every year craftspeople apply and are accepted or rejected. Few craft shows have a tenure policy, so it was difficult to plan my calendar for the coming year. Also there's an unusual amount of work entailed in merely applying. In addition to the written application, I had to send high quality slides of my work. That meant choosing the samples of my work, having them professionally photographed individually and in groups, developed, and mounted. From that batch, I would select five slides which best represented my work and made for a pleasant collection. Jurors view all five slides at one time projected on a screen. Applicants know exactly how the five slides will appear on the screen—as a pyramid, with two on the top and three on the bottom—

and must arrange their slides accordingly, balancing color and composition for optimal aesthetic viewing.

Moreover, until I was accepted at a show, I wouldn't begin production of those items, or create any promotional materials. And, given the uncertainty, I couldn't really plan anything for the coming year. I couldn't take classes or sign up to teach classes. During these waiting periods, my life was on hold. Trips to the post office were filled with angst. Behind that tiny metal door of my box lay my fate. Waiting for the thick or thin envelope was emotionally draining. I had to psych myself up before inserting my key into the lock, telling myself to remain calm even if I was rejected.

The best craft show I ever participated in was Crafts at the Castle. I was accepted the first year I applied, had the best sales I'd ever experienced, and was deliriously happy exhibiting among some of the finest craftspeople in the country. For three years running I was accepted there. On the fourth year I was rejected. It was my worst post office trip of all time. It gave me second thoughts about where my career was heading. Did I really want to spend the next decade worrying about my future in the parking lot of the Saugatuck post office?

Part of my evolution from exhibiting craftsperson to textile designer to professional speaker was spurred by not wanting external forces like a jury to decide my fate. I wanted more control over my own destiny and got it.

L E S S O N   3 8

Take it to the next level. Invest time to create systems for your business that will save time in the future.

The first time I typed a web address into a document in my newly updated Word program, I was mystified when it turned blue and became a link to the Internet. I thought it was wonderful and asked my computer teacher how it had happened. He explained, "It just knows." And I wanted to know how many years and how many technicians it took to arrive at the "it just knows" level of excellence.

By comparison, my progress always feels like a glacier, a slowly moving great weight. When I first began teaching Ukrainian Easter eggs, I would gather small groups around a table and take an egg out of the carton to illustrate ways to divide its surface. I held up a variety of decorated eggs and explained how the symbolic drawings would attract prosperity, fertility, and long life. I lit a candle and demonstrated step by step how to apply the wax and dye to the eggs.

I began to run into problems when I realized that half the eggs I had planned to use for illustration in an upcoming class had been sold, and that the group was getting too large for everyone to see the process I was demonstrating. I loved the warmth and intimacy of small classes, but wanted to teach larger numbers of people. The opportunity to make some changes came when I received an invitation to conduct a workshop at the Cooper Hewitt Museum in New York City. Teaching in the Big Apple would require a new standard. I felt as if I were going public for the first time.

It took me weeks of daily preparation to get ready for the class. I had to decide exactly what I wanted to show the class, create the eggs that would provide the designs, symbols, and history I wanted to illustrate, and then hire a photographer to make slides of my choices. Further, I needed photographs of my hands demonstrating each step in the process. Then I had to create the accompanying text so I would know, word for word, what I wanted to say.

When I delivered that first class in New York City, I read from a script with a line-by-line description of each of the traditional patterns I projected onto the screen. With practice and experience I was able to use a handful of 3x5 index cards to jog my memory. Eventually I knew the script by heart. Today, when I give a talk like this, the preparation takes about fifteen minutes, including loading everything into the car.

A few years ago I read *The E Myth Revisited* by Michael Gerber. What I devised for the Cooper Hewitt experience is similar to what Gerber recommends. Invest time to create systems for your business that will allow it to be duplicated or franchised. I'm not looking for franchises, but his advice is also applicable when I need to repeat something over and over again.

LESSON 39

Keep talking to various experts
until you reach the perfect solution.

The life of every entrepreneur is filled with peaks and valleys that often occur on the same day, if not the same hour. It's the nature of owning your own business. The trick is to be able to remember what the peaks looked like when you're in the valley. As I pursued Faith Ringgold's million-dollar idea for a dozen eggs in a glass carton, I peaked and dipped often. Initially I envisioned the eggs as similar to fine china. Those elegant designs on fine dinnerware that used to be painted by hand are now done almost exclusively with decals. Once I got over my prejudice about decals, I was able to accept the idea that they might prove useful in my work.

First I tracked down a person a friend suggested as someone who knew how to make decals. I drove to his shop in northern Connecticut and spoke to him at great length about producing decals and the transfer process. After I described the requirements, he referred me to an associate who worked closer to my home and had the sophisticated equipment I needed. I scheduled an appointment with his associate. He was intrigued with the idea of a collection of eggs and admired my designs. He took me on a tour of the premises and introduced me to the artisans he would involve in the project. I came home elated. I called in a progress report to my business coach who was walking me through this undertaking. I had agreed to research three service providers, but felt certain I'd already found the perfect person. She prodded me to check out at least one other vendor.

I dug into my Rolodex and called an art director who warned me to steer clear of the businessman I'd just met, "You've got to use our guy in New York. He's the best." So I scheduled an appointment to chat with her guy. He, too, liked the idea. Although he could also supply the decals, he thought it would be more viable to batik real chicken eggs using the traditional Ukrainian technique. He knew of a studio in the Far East that could imitate my work so closely that I wouldn't be able to tell the difference. I bought his idea.

After anxiously waiting eight weeks to see the sample from overseas, I received a package with three beautiful Chinese boxes nestled in tissue paper. I eagerly lifted the lid off each box and recoiled in disappointment. The reproduction of my designs was grossly inaccurate, and the colors were not only mismatched—they were also hideous. I was sick to my stomach and called to tell him the deal was off.

Earlier in my career I would have given up at this point, but I now have methods for dealing with these valleys. I used my coach, my mastermind group, and my friends to vent my frustrations on. And then I continued my quest. I believe that the reason the first two venues didn't work out was that there was a better option waiting in the wings.

I called Artoria Limoges, the largest manufacturer of porcelain in the world. I knew and respected their work, and originally had wanted them for the project, but was too scared to approach them. Toughened by my previous attempts, I realized I had nothing to lose. Plus I had gained a great deal of knowledge in those forays. Artoria loved the idea and helped me decide that painting my designs by hand on porcelain eggs which could be opened like boxes would be the method of choice. The Circle of Life Collection had its debut at the 2000 New York Gift Show, held at the Javits Convention Center in New York. It featured six of my quilt-patterned designs, hand-painted on egg-shaped porcelain boxes packaged and displayed in a clear carton.

CHAPTER 4

Surprises

Before caller ID I could never let the phone ring without picking it up. Who knew? Maybe the call would change my life—a fabulous order, a new client, an opportunity to appear on Oprah. One of the best parts of having your own business is that at any moment on any given day a phone call, an e-mail, or a chance meeting can shift everything. And it did. An unexpected call from the White House in 1980 improved my credibility factor overnight. A four-page spread of my work in a national magazine also helped my credibility. Networking at a national conference turned into an international speaking opportunity. When you keep showing up for your business, surprises will keep it interesting.

L E S S O N   4 0

The business plan is not as important
as the process of creating it.

As a child I believed that if you were truly grown up, you would know how to speak French and how to drive a stick shift. I thought that rite of passage to adulthood was restricted to people with these skills. Similarly, as a young entrepreneur I believed that having a business plan was the great delineator between dilettantes and successful business owners. I was a dilettante. Not that I wasn't successful—I just didn't feel legitimate or grown up as an owner of a business, and when anyone asked me if I had a business plan, I used to dodge the issue by saying, "Sure—it's in my head." My plan was to make more money. My method was to participate in more shows—I had never taken the time to go beyond these two statements.

It was finally the act of creating a business plan that made me into a businesswoman, an entrepreneur. I did one as homework assigned in a course for women business owners. In some ways the process was easier than what I had imagined. Since I had been in business for nearly a decade, I had most of the information at hand. All I needed to do was organize my thoughts and put them in writing. I also needed to spend time thinking—a rare luxury for a business owner who doesn't schedule contemplation into her daily routine. I had to ask myself the following simple questions that were very hard to answer. Who was my competition? Who was my market? What products and services was I offering or planning to offer in the future? Et cetera.

When I was finished, I shared my plan with my classmates. No one else had completed the assignment, and the whole class regarded me with awe. I, too, was awed. My self-esteem had risen several notches, and I really appreciated transition to a kind of adulthood. I had gone through a step-by-step self-examination that helped me become more aware and directed as a business owner. No, it didn't bring me instant success. It did provide me with a foundation that led to future success. Yes, a business plan is wonderful, it will make the navigation easier, but it isn't the journey.

LESSON 41

Create a resume as though you were applying for a job. You'll be impressed by who you are.

When my children were very young, I used to pore over the classified ads. I can see now that I was tempted, I wanted to look for a way to escape my life as a stay-at-home mother. I thought if I could pull in a big salary, I could rationalize leaving the nest.

Before I became a mother, I had been a high school art teacher. After that I kept my hand in the art world by exhibiting my work once or twice a year and teaching art classes in my home. But it was hard work moving all the toys to transform the play area into an art studio/classroom twice a week. And having eight more children drawing and painting in my house was exhausting. A job outside the home seemed particularly glamorous.

One day an ad caught my eye. A company wanted someone with art experience and a degree in education. I thought, "Perfect! I'm it!" The salary was $40,000, a hefty sum back then. It would justify my exit from full-time motherhood. I pictured myself going to the interview in a stylish new suit and pumps, and impressing them with my expertise.

Because I had been out of the job market for many years, I thought that it would be prudent to get help with my résumé. I met a counselor at my alma mater and described my situation—at home with three children, running an art program, and exhibiting my work at craft shows. "Why on earth do you want to leave such a good life," she said. She was envious that I was able to work part-time and be at home with my three children. She made it seem that I had what everyone wanted. I never thought that what I had at home was so special.

However, I still wanted to pursue the administrative job, and she helped me write my résumé. Actually, she transformed my credentials into something remarkable—a technique I have adopted in my business. "In addition to your craft work, what else have you been doing in the art field since you had children?" "Oh, I started having some kids come over to my house after school to help them with their drawing and painting." She translated it, "You run a community-based art program." My self-esteem began to rise. "I won a blue ribbon at a local craft fair." "Award-winning artist," she wrote in my file. My heavens, my spirits rose—She's right. I really do have an exciting life.

I believe the universe supplies us with everything we need for our growth, including stones we use to step on and rocks we stumble over. The meeting with that counselor helped me understand what I already had and what I valued most.

Luckily, I never made it to the interview stage.

LESSON 42

Driving to the correct conclusion of a problem is marvelous. And it's also wonderful to be recognized for your work.

"Hello, my name is Steve Jobs," the voice on the phone said. "I'd like to buy some of your eggs." If I got that call today, my heart would start pounding a mile a minute. I would visualize a skyrocketing bank account and start speculating how I could incorporate his name in future ads. But that call came in 1991 before I owned a Macintosh computer or even heard of Steve Jobs.

He discovered my eggs when they appeared on the cover of the Flax Art and Design catalog that was mailed to 1.2 million people in the United States. I had won a contest sponsored by Flax. It all started on a hot, sticky summer day when my assistant, Jodi Fisher, handed me a mail order catalog. The cover caught my eye. It featured a cartoon of a white Holstein cow with an abstract-looking black mark covering its torso. On closer examination, it turned out to be the Flax logo—the letter "F." Jodi told me the catalog company was sponsoring a contest for a cover design incorporating the letter "F" and suggested that we enter.

It was one of those great ideas that inspire an immediate rush of brainstorming and enthusiasm, followed by hours and weeks of hard work, second-guessing, and self-criticism. Jodi drew up a sketch which would have been brilliant if we could have produced it. We simply couldn't get the concept to work. It was aggravating and disappointing to spend all that time, energy, and resources, and get nowhere. It's also not unusual.

We loved the idea of integrating the "F" in an intricate egg pattern. We still wanted to enter the contest. Out of frustration and the upcoming deadline I came up with a simple, yet elegant solution—row after row of my quilt design eggs, with one featuring the "F" in black and white within the quilt pattern. My good friend, Carmine Picarello, photographed it, and we mailed it in just before the deadline. Three months later we learned we had won first prize.

Staying with your inspiration from inception through completion is always more challenging than you can imagine, but the rewards are marvelous.

L E S S O N   4 3

Pursue your goals systematically.
You will get where you want to go,
but not necessarily the way you planned.

I joined the National Speakers Association and was told that Marcie, the teacher of beginners in the field, was outstanding both for her knowledge of the professional speakers marketplace and the entrepreneurial marketplace. I drove five hours twice a month for these sessions—once to meet with my class with Marcie and a second time to meet with the chapter as a whole to test our new skills.

Marcie's challenge was to help us find our way in the world of professional speakers. We spent hours discussing speech topics in our areas of expertise. Determining target audiences was a major challenge, then developing marketing materials for those audiences. I was thinking of targeting the education market with my topic: *Turning Your Passion Into a Business.*

Every month we would bring in our latest marketing materials for feedback and suggestions. I brought along a sample letter that my graphic designer had formatted. My letter gave my qualifications and topics I was qualified to talk about. It was addressed to the fine arts department chairs at liberal arts colleges. I offered to inspire—for a fee—students who were considering turning their talents into businesses, as I had. They were my target audience.

Marcie and the group liked what I'd written and my promotional kit containing press clippings, testimonials as to my competence, and my bio.

I sent that letter to thirty colleges, and even though Marcie and my group loved it, it turned out to be a dud. I received one polite rejection while the other twenty-nine chairs ignored my phone calls. It took months to pursue this lead, and I got nowhere. But my enthusiasm for marketing and the quality of my materials had caught Marcie's eye. When a colleague asked her if she knew someone who could conduct marketing seminars, she suggested me, and I got the job.

I had lunch with Nancy Michaels, the principal of Impression Impact, a company that provides seminars for major corporations. She hired me to conduct a marketing seminar, *How to Be a Big Fish in Any Pond,* at the Staples store in Kalispell, Montana. Since May, 1998, I have been happily delivering programs for Nancy all over the United States.

LESSON 44

Enjoy the ride, but don't let the ride drive you.

In the early 1980s, I knew I had made it when the phone rang in my studio and it was the White House. I was sure I was on the road to fame and fortune. I was invited to decorate an Easter egg for the annual Easter Egg Roll the following spring. What more could anyone ask? This news was carried in the local papers and has followed me since. It was a boon to my career and improved my credibility. But it was not the be-all and end-all.

Have you heard of the song *Big Nuthin* by The Roches? The sisters who sang this song were invited to perform on Johnny Carson's Tonight Show. It was the biggest break any entertainer could dream of. The day came, they appeared, and nothing happened. No ringing phones, no multi-record contracts or million-dollar signings. They wrote *Big Nuthin* as a response to their disappointment. My friend Cookie, a successful children's book illustrator, had the same letdown after her New Yorker cover failed to ring any bells.

I've had many such disappointments. In fact, there is a direct correlation between my expectations and what happened. The bigger the expectation, the bigger the letdown. There was a two-page spread in a glossy magazine that I was sure would bring me orders and fans by the hordes. I received one order. Another national magazine placed a beautifully done article about me in their January issue. It arrived in households about a week or two before Christmas when reading magazines is low priority, and few sales resulted.

On the other hand, when I do have a big hit, a funny thing begins to happen. After a four-page spread in the April, 1990, issue of *Country*

Home appeared, mail started to pour in and the orders flowed. It was exhilarating. For a while there, I felt as though I was the center of the universe. Sometimes, and I hesitate to say this, it almost feels like too much attention, like I wanted to fade back into a little obscurity.

When I got married, it felt as though the whole world was focused on me. My picture was in the paper. I felt celebrated, but at some point I also felt a certain lack of privacy and freedom. People called fairly regularly to ask about my wedding plans, then about how the wedding was, and then how the marriage was.

Not too long afterward, I became pregnant and again felt like the sun in my universe. "Did you have the baby yet?" "Oh, you had the baby!" "How was the delivery?" Then came loads of gifts, thank-yous, and visits by friends and family. I wondered if it would ever end. And then, it did. Daily life took over, and I wondered where all those people went. While I savored the privacy, a part of me felt the absence of all that attention.

While those hits came out of the blue, I now choose to make them happen. This is where balance comes in. It's exciting for a business owner to be featured in any capacity—winning an award, being profiled in the newspaper, or appearing on TV. People are thrilled for you. But after a while, it becomes somewhat ordinary. The first time I appeared in the newspaper, a dozen or more people sent me clips. Now, after years of publicity, barely anyone takes the time. The message is clear. Enjoy the attention while you get it, but know it can't last.

L E S S O N   4 5

Realize that the support you get from your family will wax and wane.

Support from my family has waxed and waned over the twenty-plus years I've been in business. Lindsey often assisted me at shows. Laura greeted customers who attended my studio sales. Buddy and Rob unloaded my van when I returned home after exhibits.

Years later I attended a design course with the internationally known quilter, Michael James. It was a three-day event. After the first all-day session on Friday, I had dinner at a Mexican restaurant with some friends who had also attended the class. At home that night, I became violently ill. It was either a twenty-four-hour bug or Montezuma's revenge. I knew I would be unable to attend the Saturday session. When morning arrived, my daughter Lindsey, then about seventeen, came into the bedroom and saw me. I explained that I had been sick all night and wouldn't be going to that class that day. "Oh?" she said with a fair amount of sympathy and concern. "Then can I have the car?"

LESSON 46

A sense of humor is helpful in learning humility.

An oversized ego has occasionally been an issue for me. For years I felt that I shouldn't have to work so hard, market so much, or donate any of my goods or services to charity. I grew up with a sense of entitlement that somehow, some way, I wasn't meant to get my hands dirty. Bad lesson. Bad message.

One day there was a wonderful half page write up about me in *The New York Times,* and several weeks afterward a woman who saw it called to order my book. I asked her how she heard about the *Times* piece. Had some friend who had seen the article called to share her passion for Ukrainian eggs? No. She explained that a friend had given her old newspapers to line the bottom of the cages she used in her kennel service. She happened to open a section of the *Times* that contained the article about me. "I actually prefer getting *The Wall Street Journal* because the paper they use is more absorbent," she said.

LESSON 47

There will be things you don't even know that you don't know until they come up.

The longer I'm in business, the more I know how much I don't know. And sometimes, I discover I don't know how much I don't know. I couldn't even have dreamed up the following experience. I did my first wholesale show one cold February weekend and took thousands of dollars worth of orders for eggshell jewelry. When I returned to my studio, I figured out a production schedule and then called my supplier. I said I would need twenty dozen duck eggshells as soon as possible. There was silence at the other end. As gently as possible, my supplier informed me that the ducks wouldn't be laying eggs again until April. Could I place the order then? Accounting for Mother Nature had never occurred to me. I needed to go back to my customers and explain the situation. I did lose several sales, but most of the people told me they would wait.

It's not just the little guys who endure these lessons. I heard someone describe a corporate blunder. An American doll manufacturer she worked for decided that they should design dolls specifically for the Europeans, since they were avid doll collectors. The dolls were magnificent, exquisitely dressed and coiffed. There was one oversight—size. European houses are much smaller than American houses. The dolls were too large for the shelves in European houses. They had to be completely reworked at a cost of millions in time, research, and materials.

L E S S O N   4 8

Go! You might meet somebody!

Typically at a craft show, customers enter my booth, get a feel for what I do, and often take out their eyeglasses from a pocket or purse to examine my work more closely. At this festival I observed one customer's unusual behavior. After glancing at the designs on the front of the brooches, she flipped them over and peered at the reverse side. After spending several minutes doing this, she asked me what material I was using to fill the concave areas of the eggshell. I went into a detailed explanation of epoxy—a resin that is complicated to use, requiring precise measurement and application. She nodded. She owned a company that packaged epoxy in pre-measured units. They were much easier to use and would improve production of my eggs. Because she enjoyed my work, she offered to swap her epoxy for my jewelry. I accepted her offer and for years have been exchanging my products for hers. It's a mutually satisfying and financially rewarding relationship.

I know when I show up—participate in a craft show, attend a networking event, or simply follow through on a commitment to have lunch with a friend—something always happens, and the universe will meet me.

LESSON 49

Oh yeah, murphy's law.

After preparing for a speaking engagement in Buenos Aires, I was sure that giving my keynote presentation later in Hartford, Connecticut, would be like falling off a log. However, I did go to Hartford beforehand to check out the room where I would be speaking. But I forgot to ask about their computer system. I had sent my disk to the organizer and assumed it was acceptable.

I arrived early the morning of my talk to do a dry run. We went through about five or six of the forty slides on the CD-ROM and saw that everything was in order. What I didn't account for are the problems you encounter when you make assumptions. My son learned in fourth grade that when you assume something, it makes an "ass" out of "u" and "me."

My speech proceeded nicely until about the twentieth slide. I used the remote to advance the slides and looked up to see a gigantic red "X" on the screen. I panicked and hit the remote again and another red "X" appeared. I had evidently exhausted the memory in the computer. I gave the rest of my talk supplemented by phrases like, "and the image you would have seen here…"

It wasn't a total disaster, but it was a painful experience.

I know now. First I always check out all equipment completely— that is do a complete dry run. I prepare as thoroughly when I am talking to five people as when I am talking to two hundred. And, whether it's the capital of Argentina or Connecticut, bring your own laptop.

CHAPTER 5

Letting Go and Perseverance

You've got to know when to hold 'em, know when to fold 'em.
—Kenny Rogers in *The Gambler*

It's as much of a challenge to know when to hold and when to fold in business as it is in cards. How long do you keep pursuing a vision? And at what point do you let a project go. The challenges keep getting more and more difficult for me, but my instinct for knowing what to do is becoming clearer.

L E S S O N   5 0

Make sure your business
suits your ever-changing lifestyle.

When some people quit their corporate jobs, they already know they're going to start their own business. While still on payroll, they researched the industry they were planning to enter, created a business plan, found their office space, and only then hung out their shingle.

Then there's the rest of us. We're the ones who ooze into entrepreneurship. When someone asks me how long I've been in business, I stall. I have a hard time pinning down the exact date. I want to explain it's a long road, kind of like boasting, the same way couples who have lived together a long time before they got married always add the cohabiting years to the married years.

Officially, I got my Sales and Use License in 1980. That's when I started to pay taxes and declare myself a business rather than the hobby label the government applies to people who don't make much money at what they do. But I'd kinda, sorta, maybe considered myself to be in business before that date. I had shown and sold my work at a craft show, conducted a workshop or two, taught adult education courses. These were the foundation of my business, what it eventually would become.

But I don't tell people I started my business in 1973 because I didn't really feel like I was in business back then. Maybe I'm afraid that they'd expect more of me if they knew I'd been in business for that long. Also it didn't feel official—real—until I got the license and started sending in quarterly taxes.

Feeling as if I was running a "real" business came in stages. When I started to recognize and be recognized by other craft artists at shows,

I began to feel like an entrepreneur, and I registered for courses to learn more about entrepreneurship. When a newspaper wrote an article about my work, I felt like a professional. Getting national press made my small company seem more real. When I got my 800 number, I decided that now I was really in business. When I incorporated in 1993, I thought, it's official now. It was a number of stages, small, incremental steps. My business incubated for years before it could withstand the rigors of the commercial world.

Would I do it differently today? Yes, if I were starting a new business. The slow way my business grew was exactly right at each stage of my life. When I had young children, the business was small. Now that my children are grown, the business is big, and I'm free to fly all over the world, and I do.

L E S S O N   5 1

You have to step out of your comfort zone, take risks, and survive the moments of dread to grow your business.

On Dr. Julie White's audiotape, she relates a story about a friend in real estate. He made a killing on a property he had bought for a song and sold for a lot of money. His friends admired him for his expertise. However, he knew better. He confided to Julie that he had lost a lot of money on several other investments, and concluded, "If lucky breaks came labeled 'lucky break,' all of us would be rich." When friends and acquaintances think I'm lucky when some publicity hits, they don't know about the dozens and dozens of difficult investments of time and energy that didn't pay off at all. Those little miracles don't just happen. They happened because I did the work.

LESSON 52

In changing what is into what can be,
we learn what we need to know.

For the most part, entrepreneurship is not easy. I have endured near-empty bank accounts, rejections, humiliation, envy, and despair. I don't like to talk about any of that. However, I find myself devouring any morsel of information written about someone else's bad experiences. I want a thorough description of how they moved out of the dumps, and moved on with their lives.

Hazelle Goodman, an actress, was reported in *The New York Times* as saying, "There's no way to say it so it doesn't sound clichéd and preachy, but you've really got to hold on to what you believe. And keep breathing, crying, getting up, and going. Breathing, crying, getting up, and going. And then, you get there." She talked about how often she wanted to quit, to leave the movie industry, especially when a prospective manager said she was talented but too dark-skinned to work on camera. When I read that article something inside me knew I too could endure—all I had to do was just keep going.

Through every painful experience I learned something about how to conduct my business and my life. In my early craft-show days I would watch enviously as the artist across the aisle was comfortable working the crowds who bought her exquisite handmade jewelry. She greeted several customers with hugs and big smiles as though she'd known them for years. She was full of enthusiasm, wrote orders continuously, and had a stunning display to boot. I grumpily acknowledged that I should try to start conversations with the people who were checking out my booth, and I started thinking about ways to make it more welcoming. And slowly over the years, I redesigned my booth. I also studied assertiveness training and took seminars and weeklong workshops in personal development, and my ease with customers increased. My products improved too. By the end of my exhibiting days I had stopped noticing what was going on across the aisle, because I was too busy—I was enjoying the success I had formerly envied.

The geisha in Arthur Golden's *Memoirs of a Geisha* put it beautifully, "I don't think any of us can speak frankly about pain until we are no longer enduring it." When I give a keynote speech now, I tell humorous stories about those early days, about my embarrassment when I stood alone in my booth for hours on end, and the audience laughs with me. They know I can speak about those painful times because I have created the results I used to envy. After the pain and suffering, learning, maturity, and eventually wisdom do come. But the light at the end of the tunnel may be too hard to recognize when we're suffering in the darkness of the tunnel. There doesn't seem to be a kinder, gentler way to get to the end of the tunnel and see the light.

LESSON 53

Plowing through the nitty-gritty details to complete each task creates big results.

One day while browsing through the self-development section at Barnes and Noble, I bumped into a friend. She asked me what I was looking for. I said I was researching the competition for a book I was thinking of writing. "Wow!" She exclaimed. "I always get a lot of great ideas, but they seem to fizzle after a couple of days. In fact, right now I'm thinking about opening a wellness center. It will have yoga classes, feng shui seminars, and a fountain two stories high in the center atrium. I can see it now." She was beaming, pleased with her dream.

"That sounds fantastic," I said, visualizing my own concept of her wellness center. "Where are you on the development right now?" "Oh, just imagining what it would be like." "Do you have a plan?" I asked. That seemed to be a difficult question for her. She looked at me, found an interesting title on the bookshelf in front of us, and the conversation was over.

Having a plan in any complex venture is essential, but breaking that plan into manageable, bite-size pieces is the key to success. (See Lesson 18: on page 33.) Then there's persistence. One of the best methods for getting where you want to go is "single-handling," a term I first heard when I listened to Brian Tracy's tape, *The Psychology of Achievement*. It is simply the ability to stay with one task from the beginning to its completion. Easier said than done.

"Billiard-ball brain" was the way playwright Katherine Kerr once described her method of attacking a tough job. That was how I operated. Let me describe a typical hour.

I need to send out an order to a customer. I go to the computer to print out the mailing label. While I'm there, I can't resist checking my e-mail. I see one from my friend Janet asking if our lunch date next week can be changed from noon until one. I switch screens to my calendar page to confirm the date and notice that I have an early afternoon doctor's appointment. I look up the doctor's office number and call to find out if I can reschedule it for a later time. His receptionist agrees, and when I go to enter that new appointment on my calendar, I hear my timer buzzing, indicating that an egg I put into the dye fifteen minutes ago is ready to be taken out. I move over to my design area and remove the egg, pleased that the color saturation is just perfect. Now, where was I?

The order I started to complete wasn't processed, and I had completely lost my momentum. This scenario has been played out repeatedly in a thousand different ways in my life. One of the hardest things for me is to stay with a task from its inception to its completion. I get bored, frustrated, depressed, anxious, and ultimately lose my motivation. I want a distraction, a high, a reward. "This isn't as good as I thought it would be" or "I can't stay on hold waiting for this character to take my call" are typical things I say to myself. To get through these difficult periods—when I see that the job is going to take longer and will be more annoying than I anticipated—I take a deep breath or two, acknowledge to myself that I am single-handling this task (and aren't I great), and move forward. The high comes at the end when I actually complete the task. No matter how mundane it is, I feel good when I finish it. Then I can move onto the next item. The big goal, the wellness center of my plans, comes into clearer focus.

L E S S O N 5 4

Learn from each experience—
positive or negative—and move forward.

"Entrepreneurs fail their way to success," said Austin Pryor, a counselor with the Service Corps of Retired Executives (SCORE). I wouldn't have wanted to hear that at the beginning of my career, but as a seasoned pro, I can smile at its truthfulness. Yes, taking a business from startup to ultimate success is not a straight path. There are twists and turns along the way, advances and retreats, and sometimes near disasters. While I've steered clear of any real disasters, I have taken a number of detours that set me back in my momentum. It's important to kiss the frog and hop on, to learn from each experience and move forward.

I sat next to Gigi Goldman at a networking event one afternoon. We established immediate rapport as we talked about my skills and hers and began to get very excited about the possibility of working together on a project. Gigi imported picture frames from overseas. She hired me to create design motifs for them and wanted to come up with a possible line to work on together.

We had several meetings to discuss themes, materials, and direction for the line. I created sketches, drawings, and finished paintings of the frame patterns. We met with a marketing person to help us position the line in the marketplace. I enjoyed every aspect of the relationship as well as the work I was creating.

The glitch came when the factory overseas was unable to reproduce the colors in the designs I painted. Rather than working with porcelain, which has its own integrity, the factory was using a less expensive ceramic mold. The quality of the finished product was below the standards that both Gigi and I expected. Ultimately, after we both spent hundreds of hours and thousands of dollars on the project, Gigi decided to pull the plug.

I have experienced several dead-ends like this in my business. You could call them failures, but along the way, they taught me what I can't do and what I'm not good at. They also have shown me which dream I need to discard and which dream I need to continue dreaming. The frame project with Gigi taught me that I love collaborating. I love the synergy of working with another creative individual. I learned that it is difficult, if not impossible, to foresee what a foreign studio would do with the samples I sent. I learned that I prefer to have complete control over the end product.

I spent several years trying to become the next Laura Ashley, but time after time I received messages from the commercial world on the outside, and from my heart and brain on the inside telling me that this was not my ultimate calling. Eventually I hopped off the design path and leapt on the professional speaking route and never looked back.

L E S S O N   5 5

Time and turnover in your industry will provide opportunities to present the same idea more than once.

"Is that one of mine?" I asked the woman who was pointing to the pin on her blouse. It looked familiar, but I couldn't quite remember making it. She nodded and told me how much she enjoyed wearing it. I took a closer look. Often, I like my work better later than when I originally made it. I'm highly self-critical, so it's delightful to see one of my creations improved by time.

My friend Mary Ellroy, owner of the company GameBird, gave this phenomenon a name: "revisiting." She is an inventor who shares her project ideas and prototypes with the members of our mastermind group. Major toy companies have rejected her seemingly brilliant concepts.

Mary has learned that there are always opportunities to revisit past inventions, assess them once more, and then demonstrate them to a fresh audience. Happily, sales often result. You could call her persistent because she doesn't take no for an answer, but the term revisiting has a nicer ring. It's casting a fresh look at work you've done, dusting it off, and exposing it to the light of day once more.

LESSON 56

Until they say, "Never call us again!" Don't give up. Keep calling.

Paper House Productions has been my favorite greeting card company for many years. They sell die-cut photographic images of American icons like the Chrysler Building, Harley-Davidson motorcycles, and Elvis, as well as cats, babies, flowers, and foods. From the first time I saw their cards in a museum shop, I visualized having images of my eggs as part of their line. In 1988 I sent a mock-up of an enlarged photograph of one of my eggs, die-cut and fashioned into a greeting card. A production assistant showed polite interest. I sent her a collection of slides for future consideration. A year passed.

We missed the Easter season, but I persevered. I went to the Stationery Show at the Javits Convention Center in New York City to meet the owner and introduce myself. He, too, showed interest and asked me to send three of my decorated eggs for him to photograph. We were getting closer. Six more months passed before he processed the images, but they didn't quite satisfy him. Disheartened, I waited another year before pursuing him again.

After completing some new designs I was excited about, I sent off another set of slides. We got further this time. We got into a licensing negotiation over the telephone. I mentioned the percentage I wanted, and the owner retorted, "Who do you think you are, the Wizard of Oz?" I was so dumbfounded by this comment and I couldn't speak for such a long time, I just hung up the phone.

A few months later I was shopping at our local stationery store and passed the Paper House Collection display. I noticed their *Wizard of Oz* collection—die-cut images of Dorothy, the ruby slippers, and the Tin Man, Scarecrow, and Lion—and realized he was being more literal than figurative. I renewed my campaign. More images sent. More trips to the Javits Center that yielded nothing.

In 1996 my book was published. I was so proud of it that I thought, "Now I'm going to be really famous. Paper House will regret that they didn't team up with me." So I sent them a copy of my book, earmarked several pages featuring my favorite egg designs, and enclosed a note that read, "Last chance!"

Three days later the firm called and ordered two of my designs. In 1997, nine years after my first letter to Paper House, my eggs were featured in their catalog in a row of note cards right next to Fabergé's.

L E S S O N   5 7

Look before you leap to conclusions.

After completing the manuscript for my first book, I was invited to North Carolina to work with the publisher and their photography staff. Step-by-step photographs of the wax-resist process required my presence. Plus, they wanted my input for other layouts.

I overbuilt my importance as a writer. I fantasized a red carpet being rolled out for my arrival à la Jackie Collins. Failing that, I was hoping for a chauffeur-held placard reading: AUTHOR. In fact, my editor, who was to meet my flight, was unexpectedly detained. I had to call upon every ounce of maturity not to whine when she arrived. I had worked too hard on myself to carry on as I once had. I had long since come to the conclusion the world owed me nothing. So the fact that the hotel didn't provide mints on the pillow before I went to bed was going to be okay with me.

Part of me had enjoyed playing the victim. Look what they've done to me again. Sigh. Long extended sigh. I used to love that role until I heard the expression "Once a victim, twice a volunteer." What? Take responsibility for what makes me unhappy? Unheard of! At one time in my career, until I was assured that a situation was perfect, I got my kicks out of finding fault, feeling mistreated. I was good at it, too. I could find lint on any collar. I might not have let you know, but I did keep a scorecard.

When I arrived at the photographer's studio in North Carolina, I had already worked with a number of photographers and art directors, who each had his or her own style. But, notwithstanding their differences, they all paid extreme attention to detail. I have stood by for what felt like hours while the perfectionist removed a mote of dust, endlessly repositioned a prop, or adjusted the light settings for the tenth time. The number of elements to be carefully considered when taking a picture seems endless.

My editor and I artfully composed my egg-decorating tools and materials to be shot as the first chapter opener—a full-page image facing the text. It looked pretty good. We cautiously awaited the art director's arrival. I steeled myself for an hour of tinkering, test shots, and reworks of the layout. She arrived late, glanced at our layout through the lens of the camera, and said, "Looks good to me." I was dumbfounded that her cursory peek was sufficient for the quality I wanted in my book. Is that really the best angle? Shouldn't we be using a tripod? I didn't show my agitation because I was the guest, the author, but on the inside, I seethed.

That night, when I went back to my mintless hotel room, I recognized that I needed to work on my attitude. I was suffering; they weren't. "God, grant me the serenity to accept the things I cannot change, the courage to change the things I can, and the wisdom to know the difference." I said the serenity prayer over and over and over again. I not only recited it, I also paid attention to the words I was saying. Either I was going to have the courage to open my mouth or I needed to accept what I could not change.

The next morning before we drove to the photography studio, the editor brought me to the publisher's headquarters. As we were waiting to say hello to various staffers, I ambled over to the library filled with the company's publications. I opened several to the credit page, checking my team of players. Each volume they had produced was magnificent. The layouts were elegant, the photographs rich and inviting.

Did my reciting a prayer affect the contents of those pages? Or did my change in attitude allow me to see my world differently? I realized that my bad attitude was a cover for my feelings of insecurity. I was afraid. I was in an unknown environment with people I didn't know, working on my life's work, my baby. My old behavior pattern had prejudiced my mind. In the end, my book was beautiful.

LESSON 58

Don't quit before the miracle.

At least once a year I get ready to pack it all in, give up, shut the doors on my business, and get a job collecting tolls on the highway. This usually happens after my phone gets quiet. Then I notice that my bank account is getting lower, and I find myself spinning my Rolodex to see what stone I left unturned. Just as I am about to scan the classifieds, at the last moment I am saved. An opportunity I sought months ago or a referral from a year earlier contacts me.

This roller coaster of emotions has been with me all my life. Most of my entrepreneurial friends tell me they go through something similar every year. It's a good thing we have each other—we can call each other up and say, "Don't quit before the miracle. You can count on it. The miracle always comes through. Just hang loose and wait."

One summer when the world seemed to have gone on vacation and my monthly sales were coming up short, the phone rang. "I don't know if you'll remember me, Jane, but I came to your studio sale last April and mentioned a project I was working on. Do you remember?" It sounded vaguely familiar. I do get prospects all the time who tell me their ideas for possible projects, but I've learned to wait for the serious offers to surface rather than pursuing these leads. "Hmmmmm," I responded. "I've just gotten my funding and would like to have you paint your patterns on my models. Are you available?" The fee for this assignment was exactly what I needed to earn for the month of July. It was manna from heaven.

These painful stretches, when we're not sure how long we can endure, remind me of childbearing. Being an entrepreneur is occasionally like being pregnant. During my first pregnancy, the Lamaze instructor told us about the stages of delivery—labor, transition, and birth. I had heard plenty about labor and birth but nothing about transition. "Transition," our instructor informed us, "is the hardest part of the process. It's painful and there is little time to rest between the contractions. Thankfully, it is also the briefest part, although it doesn't feel that way." Transition is the stage when the labor room nurses get cursed at and mothers say, "I can't do this." Sounds a lot like what I go through when I can't see my next opportunity over the horizon. I want to quit, it's painful, and I'm angry. The advice to women in labor, other than doing pelvic tilts, also applies to anxious business owners: concentrate on relaxing, use visualization, and stay focused on the goal. In other words, have faith and carry on.

LESSON 59

When you have a problem and have trouble finding an answer, persist in your search. It's worth it.

I was having trouble trying to find a glass box, like an egg carton, to contain my painted eggs. At one point, I thought I had the problem licked. I schlepped to the farthest reaches of Brooklyn to locate an outfit that could fabricate these cartons in glass. And just as I was feeling triumphant—I hadn't given up, I'd done my best, and I'd found a person who was competent and enthusiastic about the project—I found out she was no longer with the company. Disaster!

Ask any of my friends who have nurtured business relationships only to find their contact has disappeared. So much energy and hope had gone into researching a company to do the job. I was so proud of myself for doing all that legwork. I wanted to scream, I wanted to give up.

For much of my life, you see, I haven't gone the distance. Maybe I was afraid I'd find no answers to my questions. Often I never even tried to find out. Sometimes I preferred to fail, rather than try harder. What kept me going in this particular journey was the support of my coach and my mastermind group. Sharing goals with a select group of individuals is an insurance policy against quitting.

In addition, the vision of my twelve eggs in a glass carton plus Earl Nightingale's watchwords—"What the mind can conceive and believe, it can achieve"—helped. Eventually, habit becomes practice. I didn't give up.

I pursued a contact I made at the Javits Gift Show in New York and contacted a Belgian who created dishes from slumped glass, a technique that seemed perfect for the glass cartons. He never returned my faxes. A prominent New England glassmaker wanted $10,000 to create a sample. An independent glass manufacturer in Manhattan was booked for the next eighteen months.

Frustrated, I still kept on going in the epic length quest for that egg carton. I attended a meeting for inventors who are traditionally generous in giving advice to other people and got the names of companies that do vacuum forming. Even though I had no idea what vacuum forming was, I trusted that these guys knew more than I did. Vacuum forming became the solution. Even though the needle was in the haystack, i.e., hard to find, I knew an answer existed. My job was to keep trying until I discovered it.

CHAPTER 6

Risk Taking and Overcoming Fear

Push the envelope.
Step out of your comfort zone.
Feel the fear and do it anyway.

Yeah, yeah, yeah. I'd already heard the mantras about taking action, but I still didn't know how to pick up the phone and call that intimidating buyer down in Texas who didn't know she was about to hear from me. How do you do that?

Sure, I look like I know what I'm doing, and I have a fairly successful track record, but I'm still terrified when a new challenge comes my way. Part of my success has come from consistently looking for higher bars to vault over.

Broken into its tiniest fragments, the way to overcome fear boils down to writing a letter, dialing the phone, putting a higher sticker price on the merchandise. More often than not, what terrifies me and a lot of other people is the anticipation before you do something and the fear that comes afterward. Actually doing the thing you are afraid of doing is often the easy part.

LESSON 60

Even experienced professionals get nervous approaching new markets.

"Would you please repeat what you just said?" the teacher Meta Schroeter asked me during my visit to her marketing class at Parsons School of Design.

I was surprised, I didn't know why she wanted me to repeat the statement, but I repeated it anyway. " I was terrified to make that call."

She turned and faced the class and asked. "How many of you were surprised to hear her say that?" Hands shot up all over the room.

"How could they not know that I was scared?" I wondered. My heart was pounding just recalling the time I phoned a prospective buyer at a particularly swank boutique. Then I realized they were clueless about my fear because I seemed so sure of myself. I had just given a forty-five-minute presentation about the history and success of my business. It was polished, professional, and confident. But as we moved into the question and answer portion of the program—the unrehearsed part—my vulnerabilities emerged. I was delighted to hear that my current audience couldn't see my fear.

I can look back on my accomplishments and feel good about them. But even though I know I have done difficult things in the past and done them well, I still am challenged daily. I wasn't always able to hide my fears. Way back when, my art appreciation program was so well received at my children's elementary school the superintendent of schools wanted to make it available citywide. He invited me to describe the benefits of the program and give a mini-demonstration to all eleven elementary school principals.

I prepared for weeks, gathering my notes, memorizing a script, and organizing posters and props. I envisioned an auditorium setup or boardroom for my presentation. Instead, the room contained simply a dozen folding chairs arranged in a circle. There was no place to hide, no lectern to stand behind. I felt too visible.

I was terrified. It was the first formal speech I had given since college. I had rehearsed in my mind, but not out loud, using a tape recorder. The principals were sufficiently interested in my content that they approved the program, but I wondered about my performance. I didn't have long to wait for feedback. The principal at my children's school, who knew me well, called me that afternoon. "It didn't sound like Jane up there." I had been so nervous my voice was an octave higher than normal.

I always appreciate hearing that performers like Sir Laurence Olivier got butterflies before performances. His supreme skill was performing spectacularly in the face of that fear.

LESSON 61

When you get an inspiration, go for it.

"Do you think," Buddy asked me, "if I wrote a detailed letter to Clinton about the legendary "Oh Hell" games Matty, Kenny, and I used to play, he would join us for a round?" My husband had recently read an *Esquire* article about Clinton and his passion for Buddy's favorite card game, a significant piece of my partner's youth. Now a retired English department chairman, Buddy could surely write a persuasive invitation.

I could easily imagine Bill Clinton getting a huge kick out of playing cards with Buddy and the guys. And now that Clinton had a home in nearby Chappaqua, New York, it would be workable. However, I wasn't sure if the letter would ever reach Clinton, and if it did, would he respond. But my husband was stymied—he wanted a guarantee before he made the effort.

Buddy's question made me realize that I used to be like Buddy. When I get an inspiration now like Buddy's, I run with it. Taking action moves me toward my wishes and dreams, and it strengthens the muscles I need for ultimate success.

I would have loved to have known in advance the answer to the question, "Do you think that Neiman Marcus will be interested in coproducing my Dozen Eggs project?" The only way to get an answer was to ask the buyer. I called her with my heart in my throat, and I found out that she wasn't interested. I wanted to hang up quickly, weep and wail, and throw the project away. Instead, I took a few deep breaths, called a good friend to whine and be comforted, then made a list of other potential buyers. Tiffany also rejected the idea of coproducing but said they might be interested in future projects after seeing how this one turned out.

All this trying and failing made me refine my dream, my attitude, and my pitch. By the time I brought it to Artoria in New York City, it was packaged in a form that interested the company enough to partner with me.

"Go for it" has become my mantra when it comes to risk taking. Too many people look back on their lives and regret that they were afraid to take a risk to achieve a goal.

LESSON 62

Trust the instinct that moved you to write a task on your calendar and follow through with it.

Did you ever get a great idea? It just comes to you and somehow you know that it's right. It goes on your to-do list. The day you appointed arrives, and you look at your list and say to yourself, "What could I possibly have been thinking? This will never work! I'll feel like a fool taking this step."

It has been my experience that if I second-guess inspiration, I lose. When I go with the initial, inspired feeling, even when I've lost the inclination, something wonderful happens. For example, I call customers ten days to two weeks after I mail off the artwork they've ordered.

As soon as I finish packing a shipment, I go to my calendar and mark a date two weeks in the future to place that call. An art professor of mine had ordered a decorated egg for his collection. I created it, shipped it, and made a note to place a follow-up call. When I saw his name pop up on my to-do list two weeks later, I had an inner dialogue that went like this: "If he really liked the egg, he would have called me. He must not have liked it. Uh-oh. Maybe I shouldn't even call. What if he didn't like my work?"

I called. His response was definitely worth it. "I've been meaning to call you. I love the egg! I'm sorry I didn't call. I'm as bad as my clients are. I hate it when they don't call me to tell me they like what I've done. I'd actually like to order a couple more."

LESSON 63

As difficult as it is, you can teach yourself to believe you deserve what you charge for your work.

I thought I would throw up. I can still recall the feeling in my stomach when Beverly Ellsley, an internationally known kitchen designer, approached me at a crafts fair in the early 1980s. She had just bought several dozen of my eggs at $35 apiece to give as gifts to magazine editors. As I was boxing them up, she said, "These should really go for $300 each."

It took me a while to understand why I got sick when she said that. My internal voice was telling me, "You don't deserve that much money for your work. You're an impostor."

However, another voice whispered, "She could be right, you know. This is quality work. This is art." But the impostor was insistent, "Who do you think you are, calling this art?" (This was years before I read The Artist's Way, which deals with the limiting beliefs many artists harbor.)

After over two decades of practicing my art, marketing my work, and nursing my personal growth, I have come to grips with the impostor and have slowly raised the selling price of my eggs from $8 apiece in 1973 to $300 in 2000 for the most ornate designs. In the early years, customers were surprised at the low prices and told me they were worth more. As I raised my prices comments like this became rarer. Now I hear customers say, "They're worth it."

They are worth it also because their commercial value has escalated as I have gained recognition for my eggs in the marketplace. I have also learned to appreciate my God-given talent to create these unique pieces. In return, I am willing to admire and pay the price for a one-of-a-kind product another artist created, knowing full well that I can't walk into any department store in the country and find a comparable piece. I also acknowledge the persistence it takes to keep plying my craft in the face of overwhelming odds against its success.

I no longer feel like an impostor for charging such prices for eggshells. I deserve it—professionally and emotionally. These prices are not arbitrary; they reflect the skill, uniqueness, and acceptance of my product.

At a recent networking event, a new acquaintance familiar with the corporate market suggested that I do seminars for corporate executives. "You could charge $10,000 for an afternoon session." Uh-oh. The same lesson in a new package.

L E S S O N   6 4

Once you're on your own,
the only person responsible for
your life and well being is you.

It's fun to make a bold move every once in a while. I took one in 1995 after I heard Kate White speak at an American Women's Economic Development Corporation conference. At the time she was Editor-in-Chief of *Redbook*. Her talk that afternoon was about gutsy versus good girls. Her message was funny and touching because the audience could relate to it easily. I wanted the women in my local networking organization to meet and hear Kate as well. Inspired by her message, I approached her after her talk and invited her to come and address my networking organization in Connecticut. She agreed.

Hearing her message a second time made me even more willing to take risks. Earlier that week my publisher sent me a mock up of the front cover of my first book. It was ghastly. It looked like the cover of a religious textbook, not like a coffee table book. I felt sick to my stomach when I thought about having to promote my work in that wrapper. Kate's talk revved my spirits, and I went out of my comfort zone, the one that would tell me it didn't matter. I called my publisher that afternoon, and he must have heard me because the cover was changed. When people ask me how I got a particular article about me in the press, or a seat at the head table more often than not, the answer is: I asked.

If we are fortunate when we are children, someone will keep an eye on us and encourage us to take advantage of opportunities that are appropriate. Once I was grown, I wondered who would say, "Jane, you really ought to meet that editor, send out a press release, or see if anyone in your alumnae group can help you out." But, once you're on your own, the only person responsible for that kind of encouragement is you.

L E S S O N   6 5

Step out of your comfort zone when someone asks you to do something that seems hard.

When I asked a new acquaintance what she did for a living, she said she was an interior designer. I was interested because I was currently redoing a bedroom in our house. I asked her several questions and wrote down some resources she recommended. As we were about to take our seats for the evening's program, she leaned over to me and whispered in confidence, "That's the first time I've ever said out loud that I'm a decorator. I've been taking courses for two years now, and it's what I really want to do." Up to that moment, I had fully accepted her for what she claimed to be. After the explanation, I began to question her recommendations.

In my early days attending networking events I would never introduce myself to someone standing alone. Instead, I would sidle up to a friendly looking cluster of women and hope that my interesting name tag—Jane Pollak, An Egg by Jane—would attract their attention. And it did. "An Egg by Jane?! What is that?" someone in the group would invariably ask, allowing me to enter the conversation. For years I worked on my response to that simple question as well as to others that came after it. A major benefit of joining a networking group is the opportunity to test your material in a comfortable environment.

After several years in the Entrepreneurial Woman's Network, I was asked to serve on the board of directors. Once you are on the board, it is assumed that you will take on any responsibility. At our May Grand Networking Event, I arrived early to set up the registration area. The president of EWN came over to me and said we were short on hostesses. Would I be willing to act as a greeter?

"What does that entail?" I stalled. "Just go up to everyone you see, introduce yourself, and start talking." It's that "just" word again. Like it's so easy. So I took a deep breath and acted as if it was the most natural thing in the world for me to do. An amazing thing happened. Everyone I approached bought me as the hostess with the mostest; I watched each woman's face brighten because of the attention I was paying her. She would open up and relax, relieved that she wouldn't have to spend the next hour examining her Filofax or rereading the program.

No one noticed I was way outside of my comfort zone. They were too wrapped up in their own discomfort. I wanted to let them in on my secret that I had never done this before and was scared. But I refrained. What's the point? Just relish the success and move on.

Stepping out as a greeter, I had the opportunity to act like a hostess. The success I had at the job gave me the confidence to try that behavior again without the assignment. And I never confessed that I had to step out of my comfort zone to do it.

It works every time.

LESSON 66

When you acknowledge that your childhood feelings are interfering with your business relationships, you can move on.

For one full year I pursued an industry I desperately wanted to buy my seminars—the egg producers of this country. It was an extensive campaign that included marketing materials, letters, phone calls, e-mails, and meetings. Finally, thirteen months after my introduction to Christine Bushway, the industry's marketing and promotions consultant, I was hired to conduct an egg-decorating workshop at a national meeting in California.

It was exhilarating. The workshop was a huge success. The group, made up of all the wives of the egg producers, loved having a session that wasn't about omelets or soufflés—the usual fare at these events. In addition, I sold egg-decorating kits, copies of my book, eggshell jewelry, and handmade ornaments. It was the perfect marketplace for me.

During the cocktail hour before the banquet, several women made a point of introducing me to their husbands and praising my program. I felt like their darling. I imagined I'd be on their roster for as long as I liked. I thought I had it made. Not so. I looked forward to being hired to give workshops all over the United States. When a week passed and I hadn't heard from anyone, I thought maybe they're just planning a more thorough itinerary for me. I continued to keep in touch with Christine. She had heard the good reports and was eager to help keep the ball rolling. A month went by. Then two months. No bookings.

I was working with a business coach during this process. I gave her weekly updates. She noticed my flagging enthusiasm. After six months of phone calls and emails, I was ready to give up. When Valerie Barone, my coach, asked me what was happening with the egg people, I barked at her, "Forget it! If they're not dying to have me come back, I'm not going to keep pursuing it."

She adjusted her coaching hat. "Jane," she prodded, "tell me again how you felt during that presentation last October." I brightened at the memory. "It was one of the most rewarding days of my life. I loved doing it, and they seemed to love me. It was fun, lucrative, and just about the best thing I'd ever been involved in."

"Can you take a moment and think about what is happening to your enthusiasm?" Fortunately, I am always interested in why I behave the way I do. I'm not always comfortable with what I uncover, but I'm usually willing to have a look. "I hate the fact that they haven't pursued me. I'm disappointed and hurt. I want to walk away from them, so they don't have a chance to walk away from me."

It was an abandonment issue dating back some forty years. It had nothing to do with the business I was running. I continued to pursue the egg people and have presented annually to them for several years.

L E S S O N   6 7

Seeing a friend transformed by illness alters your definition of what a challenge is.

It was a cool spring morning when I drove to the rehabilitation center to see my friend Milles who had a brain-stem stroke. Her family said she was recovering well and in good spirits. I had received a picture postcard of her sitting in a garden, and the mailing appeared to be in her handwriting.

The door to her room was slightly ajar, so I tapped lightly and entered. I was unprepared for what I saw next—she was strapped in a wheelchair, one eye turned in my direction, the other unfocused in another direction. The top of her warm-up suit was covered with food stains.

When she spoke to me, it was difficult to understand what she was saying. She had to repeat each word over and over until I could decipher it. Her mind was still brilliant, but her ability to communicate was severely impaired—it was agonizing for her and frustrating for both of us.

Her son Brennan arrived a while later and gave me a full history of her recovery. She had been unable to speak at all immediately following the stroke. With frequent therapy and enormous persistence, she had worked up to the level I saw that day. Forming words were a major effort—getting sufficient breath to pass over her vocal cords was a daily challenge. After an hour or two, I left, humbled by the vicissitudes of life and their effects on my friend.

Not long after my visit with Milles, I picked up an issue of *People* that gave a full report on Christopher Reeve's recent appearance at the Academy Awards. It was his first appearance in public since the accident a few months before that had destroyed his spinal cord. The article described a spasm Reeve suffered right before he was wheeled in front of the TV cameras. His entire body involuntarily had folded in half. He had to be physically pried back into a seated position to face the public.

I wondered what I could learn from both these people without diminishing the awful thing that had happened to them. Why did they both cross my path in so brief a time? Two thoughts immediately came to mind. I realized that there is a great deal I take for granted in my daily life. Being able to breathe easily and form words clearly is not something I thank the universe for on a daily basis. Being able to move my body each day never seemed like a gift. I also realized how often I paralyze myself in my work. Given the ability to speak, to think, and to act, I will still choose not to make the effort.

At this time I was working as a textile designer. As a result of my new realization of how lucky, and how simple the challenges facing me were compared to Milles and Christopher Reeve, I decided to go to New York to walk through the Decoration and Design Building. I had my portfolio with me and offered to show it to the art director of a well-known carpet manufacturer. I had dreamed about designing for a company like his, but never had the courage to make the call.

He warned me before he took my portfolio, "If you design florals, we've got all we need." I answered, "My designs are mostly geometrics." However, after thumbing through my prints he looked up and said, "These are exactly what we've been looking for." That immediate reinforcement of a new behavior became a touchstone I refer to whenever I find myself stalled. When I remember Milles and Christopher Reeve I am encouraged to fully utilize my God-given gifts each day.

LESSON 68

To avoid feeling like an impostor,
work through all the developmental stages first.

Ridgeway Elementary School had two entrances for us children. Kindergartners through third graders entered through the left-hand doors, fourth through sixth graders through the right. I still remember crossing over that invisible line one morning. I had something to tell my older sister, who was standing with her friends on the right side. "What are you doing over here?" she sneered at my invasion into her sacred space.

That didn't scar me for life, but after repeatedly invading her space, something she couldn't stand, I began to worry about moving into a space where I didn't belong. It left me feeling that I had to earn the right to be anywhere. I know other kids hop right up to the plate, but I'll bet they're kids at the top of the pecking order—they were born first.

As a college freshman, I looked up to the seniors. I wondered how they got to be so mature, so all knowing, so...old. When I became a senior by going through the same process all seniors go through—I couldn't fathom why those freshmen were looking up to me.

After several years of exhibiting my work, I felt I had earned the right to apply to Boston's Crafts at the Castle, the Mecca of craft shows. After thorough preparation and hours of travel, I reached my destination, set up my booth, and walked around the exhibit hall to look for familiar faces. I saw only sixth graders.

Eventually, the "big kids" worked their way around the show and took a look at my work, too. They admired my eggs and jewelry.

Several offered to barter goods with me—the ultimate compliment. I felt accepted.

In *Rules for Being Human,* rule number six says "There" is no better than "Here." When your "There" has become "Here," you will simply obtain another "There" that will again look better than "Here."

I now understand where my "here" and "there" are and what keeps me from moving from one to the other. I acknowledge it as my process and go step by step or even skip a grade, depending on the situation.

CHAPTER 7

Customer Service

It's a piece of cake to describe how I like to be treated as a customer. I want to be taken care of. I enjoy being spoken to with courtesy and respect. And I prefer to get my way. When that happens, I tell the world about my experience. When I receive poor service—when I'm kept on hold, told there's no record of my order, when I'm ignored—I become ornery. And I tell the world about my experience.

As an entrepreneur, I find it an enormous challenge to provide good customer service. It means working harder, not making as much money, and sometimes admitting I've made a mistake. But I know that just like me, my customers will tell the world about their experiences.

L E S S O N 6 9

Build your reputation
one customer at a time.

Once I ordered a richly patterned wool challis scarf from a catalog company. When my shipment arrived, I was disappointed when I found the scarf was made of rayon. The colors were not as vivid, and the fabric lacked the texture I anticipated. I thought I was going to have an unpleasant time over the phone with the customer service department, but I left the conversation not only satisfied but also astonished by their attitude.

They asked me, "How can we make you happy?" What a concept–to ask the customer what she wanted. I told the representative I was disappointed because I had ordered the scarf to wear as an accessory while exhibiting my work that weekend. "Why don't you wear the one we sent you and then return it to us after the show?" the customer service representative suggested.

I felt they were really taking care of me.

I want my customers to feel the same way. So many businesses act defensively offensive when a customer complains. I had been guilty of that myself. Although I've mentally blocked out the specifics of past experiences, I still remember giving the evil eye to one customer who was browsing in my booth. She held up a blackened finger to show me that the epoxy I had used on the pin on the back of a brooch hadn't dried sufficiently. I wanted to blame her. Call it immaturity, human instinct, or self-defense, anything but customer service. I resented her calling attention to my inadequacy so much I didn't even offer her a tissue to clean her finger.

Another example of a company that knows how to provide customer service is Stew Leonard's, the world's largest dairy store. They are just two miles from my home, so I get to witness its operations on a frequent basis. In the store's front entrance is an enormous rock into which is chiseled the company's two-rule philosophy: The customer is always right. If the customer is wrong, go back to rule number 1.

I remember the first time I consciously tried this approach. A woman who had bought one of my pins called me a week or two after its purchase. "Some of the shiny coating on my pin has chipped off," she said. "No problem," I replied. "I'll send you another one and enclose a return mailer for yours." That didn't hurt too much. It so happened I had a duplicate piece in my inventory and could easily replace the damaged pin. I felt that I had handled a customer complaint gracefully. One month later the same customer phoned again. "Jane, I'm very upset to tell you this, but I'm noticing a similar occurrence on the replacement pin. The shiny coating is peeling off." My instinct was to bark, "What are you doing to my pins?" But, because I had played the role of frustrated consumer many times myself, I wanted to handle her complaint with grace and ease. I explained that I had no more of that design in stock, but that I would be happy to make a new one and send it to her. The epoxy fillings and coatings each take twenty-four hours to set, so the process is labor intensive and time consuming. But I had vowed to make my customers happy. Within a week I had completed the new version of her order and shipped it off. She called me as soon as she received it. "You have the best customer service I've ever experienced," she said.

I had no idea what to expect when I followed through on my commitment to take care of my customers. She helped me learn a valuable lesson. I create my reputation as a business owner one customer at a time, the same way that Stew Leonard and the catalog company create theirs. Caring for each and every customer is an indispensable duty.

Good customer service benefits me in another way. For instance, I called the epoxy manufacturer to find out how to get better adhesion in the future, and with the information they gave me, I became a better, more informed artisan.

L E S S O N   7 0

Not every financial outlay
will yield visible revenues.

Faced with items that textile designer, Ryl Norquist, felt were either not up to her high standards or simply didn't sell, she made the decision to reduce the price to slightly above cost. Ryl labeled this practice as part of the cost of doing business. It was the first time I'd heard that expression. At that time, I had only owned my company for a few years, and I believed that every nickel I spent had to generate a reasonable net return. If it didn't, I feared I might not be profitable.

Not all of my handwork emerges as first-quality goods. I can execute the same design a dozen times in a row and have eight pieces that come out perfectly, three that are fine if you squint, and one that doesn't meet my quality control specifications. The dye didn't take properly; the epoxy topcoat came out cloudy. There are always one or two items that don't pass muster. The question is what to do with them. Having a seconds sale, as Ryl did, benefits my customers—many are thrilled to purchase my work at a discounted rate—and it benefits me, because I salvage some of time/money spent in doing the work. Similarly, in my speaking career I have given many pro bono talks when empty squares filled my calendar. I have absorbed the cost of travel, handouts, and marketing materials for these events.

The bottom line is that practices like this ultimately benefit your company. For instance, I have given many free speeches and made many sales because of these speeches. Or after a free speech, people may come up to chat and in the ensuing conversation will refer me to other people who can help me in marketing my work. Not every dollar you spend can be directly correlated to sales. However, you can create good will among select customers by inviting them to shop at reduced prices or by giving away your products or services. Benefits come down the line, and you begin to recognize the value of spending money to make money—it's the cost of doing business.

L E S S O N 7 1

Listen to customers' complaints.
It will pay off.

"You want to write off your trip to Universal Studios?" my accountant asked incredulously. "Yes," I replied. "While our intention was to have fun there, it turned into an opportunity to do some research."

My husband and I went there on a hot, dry summer day—at least ninety degrees in the shade. Lines at the park snaked around the maze of holding pens. Every ride we passed was equally mobbed, so we chose the "E.T." line. Most of the great theme parks have figured out how to keep the folks happy during the long waits. They sprayed us with water, not heavy enough to drench us and our clothes, just a delicate spray.

"Can you imagine the courageous employee who made that suggestion?" I pictured the company meeting where one disgruntled employee after another complained about how poorly treated they were by customers who had grown hostile in the long, sweltering lines. "Why don't we just pour water on 'em and cool 'em down?" I also knew that it must have taken months of analysis, planning, and implementation.

The ride was fun, but it was the fabulous customer service that stayed with me. What lengths do I go to for my customers? What did they think? What didn't they like? I think about details like this in my work as both a keynote speaker and artist. When I first started making pins out of eggshells, I attached the pin backs and earring posts with sticky pads. Too many were returned with that piece missing. My customers were gracious because they loved the jewelry, but I knew I needed to improve the pins. I now embed the pin backs and posts in a second layer of epoxy, increasing the production time by twenty-four hours but creating a permanent solution. Of course, new buyers don't even notice the improvement. That's good customer service.

Much as I dislike hearing criticism, no matter how gently couched, I now regard it as an opportunity to keep my customers cool.

L E S S O N   7 2

Constructive feedback from customers will make you a better entrepreneur. Accept it with grace.

On a recent shopping expedition to my local supermarket, I was annoyed by the poor selection of fruit. I thought of simply telling the store's buyers that the fruit was lousy, but I know that's not really helpful. It's too vague, and people tend to dismiss the cranky customer. I needed to put a little thought into my suggestion. I told the store via the suggestion box that I like large, unblemished, beautiful fruit and vegetables, and their fruit didn't meet that criteria. When you criticize a service, a store, a manufacturer, it's best to be precise, or they will not know what you really are talking about.

The owner of a speakers' bureau came to hear my first paid speech. Although she said she loved my talk and knew the audience did too, she used two words that helped me decide that we probably shouldn't work together. She said my introduction sounded canned and that one example I used was trivial. I know I'm sensitive, but there are ways of telling people they need improving without hurting them. I prefer criticism I find constructive rather than destructive.

L E S S O N   7 3

It is important to thank everyone who
has helped you in significant ways.

When we were growing up, my brother teasingly referred to the Dow Joy Averages—the family's measuring device for how much credit we brought to the family on a given day. It made me hyperaware of who owed me what and whom I owed what. When I teach strategies for growing your business, I always include thanking people who have helped you in significant ways. I don't mean thanking the people who hold a door open for you. I do mean showing your gratitude when someone gives you a great lead or referral, a piece of advice, or has simply said something that has helped you grow your business.

Although most people don't keep score, they do have an unconscious accounting system that registers if there are still "open emotional accounts receivable." You can only withdraw as much as you have put in.

Once I was telling a class in a college about the evolution of my business. One of the students was interested in the construction business. As I had a friend in the construction business, I suggested that the student call him. About six weeks later I phoned my friend to check out an upcoming conference. When my student answered the phone, I was very surprised and asked what he was doing there. He replied, "Oh, I'm working for Mark now." Neither one had acknowledged that I had put together their relationship. All that is required is the simplest line in the mail—"thanks so much for the referral"—or a quick phone call. That little touch can work wonders.

LESSON 74

Stay focused on the people
who are buying your products.

I go often to a day spa I like and talk frequently to the owner, Noel. She nurtures her customers and they respond by caring about her and her spa. I asked her how she started her business. She answered simply, "The owner of a beauty parlor handed me a broom and said, 'First you will sweep hair. Then you cut hair.'" Noel is one of several successful women who inspired me. Her humble beginnings, her spiritual approach, and her use of feng shui—everything she says interests me. As marketing ploys, she gives a $5.00 gift certificate to each customer and a reduced price on haircuts for customers who make appointments at hours when the spa is slow. I took her up on both offers. I used the $5.00 for my first haircut, and since I don't work a 9 to 5 job, I get my hair cut on Tuesday mornings and save even more money.

The spa is also very efficient. You can tell from the moment you walk in. The first time I went to the spa, the receptionist consulted the computer, "I see you're here for the first time. Let me show you where we keep our smocks." And she escorted me personally to the dressing room. On the way, she asked, "While you're waiting for your shampoo, can I bring you a cup of coffee, tea, herbal tea, or hot water with lemon?" She made me feel pampered, treasured, wonderful.

A bit later when I emerged with my smock on, a young man dressed in black approached. "I'll be giving you your shampoo." And he too escorted me personally to my chair. Once there, he asked, "May I massage your neck and shoulders while we wait for the water to warm up?" I felt like a goddess.

I haven't even mentioned the feng shui of the salon. The layout is absolutely functional. At the same time it is breathtakingly beautiful with a unique array of building materials, textures, and fabrics. It makes you feel good to be there.

The haircut was equal to every other part of the experience. For Noel's five-dollar investment, I became a regular customer. She further endeared herself to me when I had a problem. After two of my appointments had been canceled because my haircutter was ill, I asked for a substitute. They offered me Armando. I arrived early so that I could check him out before he cut my hair. He had a very attractive blonde in his chair and was fussing over every strand on her head, smiling and laughing. I couldn't wait to sit in Armando's chair. When it was my turn, I offered Armando a photograph of myself showing him the cut I wanted. He acknowledged it with a nod and proceeded to work. Throughout the thirty minutes in his chair, he did not say one word to me. I felt invisible, unimportant, and embarrassed. When I paid the receptionist, she asked me how everything was. "Not as good as usual," I muttered almost inaudibly. "Someone will call you," she responded immediately. (Noel's staff is very sensitive to customer complaints.) The next day I received a call from a person on staff. She listened to me vent. The haircut the haircut Armando had given me was fine. It's just that it wasn't how I like to be treated. "We would like to make it up to you," she said. "Can we give you a complimentary visit?" "No," I protested. "You've already exceeded my expectations by hearing me vent. I'm okay now. Thank you." I felt important and valued as a customer. What impressed me even more was that within a week of that follow-up call I received a handwritten letter from Noel promising to make my next appointment "nothing short of perfect." Every detail of Noel's business, from the towel rack in the ladies room to the talent of her practitioners, has her personal stamp.

CHAPTER 8

Listening and Passion

"A little birdie told me…" The phrase is more acceptable than "I listened to my inner voice." Some people are just not ready to hear about a higher consciousness, and I'm not completely comfortable writing about such a thing even though I believe in it. I first started to think that the universe might hold a plan for me when bumper stickers looked as big as billboards, and songs on the radio grabbed my attention. Maybe these were not merely coincidences. Maybe there was a path I was meant to be on. Fighting that path over the years only intensified the universe's call for my attention. Now that I am faithfully pursuing the work I was intended to follow, the messages are no longer so loud.

L E S S O N   7 5

When you show up and do the footwork,
the universe clears a path for you.

When inspiration strikes, I make a commitment to a specific date, like
"research entrepreneurial associations at the library" or "call the CEO
of XYZ Corporation." It's painless to write the action on a calendar.
That's why I do it first—to ease my way into the harder part.

The challenge comes when that day arrives and my assignment is
due. I had promised myself to make travel arrangements to attend a
valuable workshop in San Francisco. I shuddered. I had to decide exactly what time I needed to leave to fly to the West Coast and come back
home. That doesn't sound so hard to do, but it's a lot harder than curl-
ing up on my comfy sofa with a good book. It also means spending a
significant amount of money.

Once I begin working through the stages to achieve a goal, invariably the universe steps in to help. That sustains me through the process.
Before I called United Airlines, I checked to see how much frequent flier
mileage I had earned. I had enough for a free domestic flight on United.
The agent on the phone told me I had 10,000 more miles than I thought,
leaving me only 105 miles shy of an upgrade to business class. No problem, he offered to credit me with those miles and debit them next time
I flew United.

Goethe described this experience in this quote I have hanging
above my desk. "The moment one definitely commits oneself then
Providence moves, too." I find myself taking on bigger and bigger challenges just to see what cool surprises the universe will move my way.

L E S S O N   7 6

The more ambitious the vision, the more arduous the journey. The harder the journey, the bigger the thrill when it is completed.

In my goal-setting workshops I use "singing arias at the Metropolitan Opera House" as an example of an inconceivable goal because I am tone deaf. But when Faith Ringgold said I should sell my eggs only by the dozen and in a glass egg carton, I knew her idea was not only a million-dollar concept but also was achievable. Thrilling *and* possible.

For me, a good goal gives me a tingly feeling in my gut, as inspiration rushes into my brain. That feeling says, "This could be yours, Jane." What remains after that initial burst of enthusiasm and delight is the achievable portion, also known as hard work. Conceivable is the fun part; achievable tells the story behind success.

"What the mind can conceive and believe, it can achieve," Earl Nightingale said. His album *The Strangest Secret* was the first spoken word recording to earn a Gold Record for selling a million copies. Its message: We become what we think about.

Over a year had passed since I'd met Faith Ringgold and had taken her suggestion to heart. I then took one step every week to move the project forward, sometimes devoting each of those days to design patterns or research manufacturing options. When the owner of Artoria saw my painted eggs in the glass carton, she exclaimed, "Outrageous!" I knew I had finished the long trek: I had heard what Faith Ringgold had to say, recognized its importance, researched the production of the glass carton until I was exhausted, designed the eggs, packed up the cardboard box containing the eggs in the glass carton, and sent it to Artoria.

I felt the thrill of success, not only in the final product, but also in the realization I had done the work. I had come through on my dream.

Visions come to all of us. Achievement is seeing the vision become reality.

L E S S O N 7 7

Trust your gut.

I visit Bergdorf Goodman, one of the most sophisticated and expensive department stores in the world, the same way I go into the Metropolitan Museum of Art. Both places display top-quality objects that are wonderful to look at, and in many cases of incalculable cost. I go to gaze, to study great design and craftsmanship, and to be inspired.

On one trip I got more than I'd bargained for. As I was taking in a showcase filled with ornate jeweled boxes, my eye became riveted to one particular design. It was an enlarged metal and rhinestone replica of one of my original intricate egg designs. A dead ringer. I got the same feeling I used to get as a child when I discovered that my sister had worn my favorite blouse to school without asking permission.

I wanted to dismiss the feeling of being robbed of something that belonged to me. Instead, I wanted to feel flattered that a well-known designer was copying me. But I couldn't get past the fact that she had copied my art without permission or payment. My gut was telling me, "Don't ignore this." But I ignored my gut because I was afraid of whatever I needed to do to set this right.

Two days later, a friend from the Entrepreneurial Women's Network called. She was an image consultant and personal shopper who spent hours combing Manhattan stores. "Jane," she said, "I was in Saks yesterday and saw your designs on some boxes there. I recognized them right away. Has someone licensed your egg designs?"

My feelings were reaching epidemic proportions. A third sighting at Bloomingdale's confirmed that I had to take action even though I didn't want to. I had never hired a lawyer and had no idea what my rights were, nor did I know how to proceed. Fortunately, at an Entrepreneurial Women's Network event that same month, I cornered an attorney and asked her for advice. She represented several creative clients and was familiar with such issues, so I hired her to handle the case.

Her first letter to the offending company was met with its complete denial of any wrongdoing. My lawyer's second letter was stronger, warning that we would bring evidence of the infringement to the stores' attention. The designer settled promptly, removed the copied pieces from the department stores, and paid my legal fees.

I received two lessons from that experience, the first one was immediate—the pleasure of seeing justice prevail. The second I learned years later: I could have handled the situation differently. I could have approached the designer and asked for recognition and payment. I could have formed an alliance with her. I still sometimes toy with the idea of seeking her out and suggesting that we work together. I think of how much I'd like to own a jeweled version of my eggs.

LESSON 78

What you do for pleasure is your passion.

How do you know if something is your passion? When I got into the car one day, I was in the middle of an audiocassette of Jane Applegate's *201 Great Ideas For Your Small Business*, and I was looking forward to hearing the rest of the tape. Some people might consider it homework, but for me it was pleasure. And then it came to me: I don't have to *make* myself listen to the rest of the tape. It was exactly what I wanted to be doing with my life. It was entertainment, not work.

Years ago, when I was taking courses in textile design at the Fashion Institute of Technology, I loved painting in class, and I loved the homework. But I had to drag myself into Macy's to check out the new fabric designs. I knew if textile design was truly right for me, browsing stores would be a priority. It wasn't. That was my first clue that maybe it wasn't the right career. I wasn't going to dethrone Laura Ashley.

No matter where I am, I have a cassette with me or business articles regarding entrepreneurship. I really don't read novels much any more, much to the chagrin of my English teacher husband. I crave accumulating knowledge about why and how entrepreneurs operate. I'm always listening to a motivational or informational speaker, the latest issue of *Voices of Experience*, or a borrowed tape from a colleague.

I've always watched what people do more closely than I've listened to what they say. I hold myself to that same test. When I hear myself or anyone else say "I really want to ——" I watch closely to see if there's some behavior to back up that dream. Otherwise, I recognize it as more of a fantasy than a goal.

L E S S O N   7 9

At any given moment, you are doing exactly what you choose to be doing, whether you admit it or not.

Talk about wearing your heart on your sleeve, how about the words on people's T-shirts? My friend Marcie Shepard mentioned one T-shirt quote that was the saddest and funniest, I'd ever heard. "I ran out of sick days, so I called in dead." So few words, yet so revealing.

Many years ago my friend Jerry was working as a short-order cook to support his family until his operatic career took off. For his birthday one year we were invited to give gag gifts. I embroidered a white chef's apron with the words, "I'd rather be singing." It got a laugh even though it broadcast his underlying angst. He wanted a singing career, but at the same time he realized he might not succeed and understood that he had financial obligations to his family.

At first I went into teaching art, rather than doing art, because I had no idea how I could make a living as an artist. I might have claimed that I would rather be painting, but truthfully I knew I would rather be working at a job with a salary, benefits, and paid vacations than figuring out how to survive as an artist. I didn't know how to do that work and was scared.

When I was a full-time mother, I occasionally voiced longings to work outside my home, but if that was what I truly desired, I could have made it happen. My real choice was what I was spending my time doing.

Once I began doing what I love, now that I am a professional speaker, artist, and author, I can't imagine I'd rather be doing anything else. Yet, I never could have gotten to this point in my entrepreneurial life without first passing through all the other stages.

L E S S O N   8 0

Success is enjoying what you've worked hard to get and recognizing you're there.

There are moments in my studio, when every action is conscious. I am pulling up my e-mail, flipping through my Rolodex, noticing the stack of mail awaiting my attention. Then there are moments when I pick up a stylus, put on my magnifying glasses, reach into an egg carton, and begin to make wax markings on the surface of the shell. I'm not aware of the time, of my breath, of anything other than the activity of my hands. My attention is on the aroma of the melting beeswax, the heft of the egg in my fingers, and the design unfolding before me. I am, as they say, in the zone.

I spend my time doing work that I love and is financially rewarding. I'm performing it in an environment that I have created in a home I love with the people I most enjoy being with. And, most important, I recognize that I have created a career that makes me happy. For me, this is success.

Yes, there are moments when the dye doesn't take, the final coating is lumpy, or the egg cracks as I'm removing its contents. There are times when piles of paper completely cover my carefully designed workspace, evenings when my husband's long hours at work are preferable to his presence in the house. I am normal.

What I have accomplished with my work and life, however, is my own definition of success. I know what I want to be doing. I've worked to a point in my life where I am doing it. I recognize that I have what I want. As simple as that sounds, I don't know a lot of people who can say this.

It takes years to achieve this simplicity and satisfaction. You'll know you're there when you no longer look over your shoulder to see what the other guy is doing, if he's happier than you, or if his house is bigger and his kids have nicer outfits.

At a mutual friend's fiftieth birthday party, I met a woman who ran a women's economic development office in northern New England. She had a difficult time believing her client when she said, she'd be happy making $20,000 a year, raising and selling her tomatoes. I understood that client exactly. To me, she is the quintessential lifestyle entrepreneur. She knows exactly what she needs to do, and her need for externals is diminished.

As my professional speaking career evolves, I find myself looking over my shoulder again. I am watching what the more successful speakers are doing, how they live and travel. I am in the awkward, self-conscious stage. And I know my choice to be a professional speaker is valid when I am in front of an audience—in the zone. It tells me that I am on the right track once again.

L E S S O N   8 1

Choose the vendors who listen to you.

A salesman came to my home office one afternoon to pitch the benefits and features of his payroll service. I had called him because I was ready to delegate another time-consuming, yet essential, task of a business owner. He strode into my space, took a look around, and began to spout his company's services. "We work with a lot of small offices like yours, we have several one- and two-man operations." "Actually," I corrected him, "this is a one-woman operation." "Yeah, yeah, yeah," he agreed.

He continued to talk about the conveniences his company offered. I could make a toll-free call each week to report my payroll. I would speak to one of twelve different employees or just leave my figures on a voicemail recording. They would handle the rest.

"What if I always want to talk to the same person each time?" "Oh, anyone at the company will be able to help you," he replied.

"Do you have some other business owners I might call for references, to see how it's working for them?" "Sure, let me give you the names of some of the ten-man and fewer businesses I deal with." Somehow I had the feeling that he was not listening to my needs and was not even noticing what kind of a company I was operating.

Fortunately, I had called two other payroll services that also sent out salesmen. I chose to work with the company whose owner came to see me. He asked me a lot of questions about my business and then addressed each of my concerns. I've been working with him for many years now and highly recommend this service to all entrepreneurs whether they're a one-woman, one-man, or a slightly larger operation.

L E S S O N   8 2

If you are able to pursue your passions, you are among the lucky few.

Eight out of ten wage earners in this country are not happy with their jobs. I'm married to one of those eight. Every morning my husband does his exercise regimen on our bedroom floor before he heads to the gym. One morning I heard mutterings coming from his direction.

"What's that you're saying?" I asked. "It's my mantra," he replied.

"I can't quite make it out," I said. "What exactly are you saying?" "I hate my job, I hate my life. I hate my job, I hate my life." Although he loves teaching, he has always detested getting up early to go to work.

"Oh." I said. Then, thinking how hard it must be for him to have a wife who is overjoyed to get up each morning, I asked, "Do you resent what I'm doing?" (Incidentally, my mantra is "I love my work, I love my life.") "I'm not resentful," he said. "I'm envious."

Time after time I read articles or attend seminars in which someone asks audience members, "Do you hate getting up in the morning?" or "How many of you wish you didn't have to go in to the office?" I never raise my hand. I always want to get up. This is a quantum change from the time I worked for someone else—like when I was teaching. I rejoiced in snow days and slept in on all holidays. Now I'm so excited by what I'm doing each day that the thought of dozing off again would mean I'd be missing some part of my day.

LESSON 83

What makes you unique makes you successful.

When I tell people that Arnold Schwarzenegger is my role model, they look at me as though I'm crazy. But Arnold's message continues to resonate for me. In an interview on TV with Barbara Walters, he said when he came to this country, he was repeatedly given three pieces of advice. He was told that no one in this country was interested in bodybuilding, that he had to lose his accent because no one would be able to understand him, and that he had to change his name, because how on earth was anyone going to remember Arnold Schwarzenegger?

Making my living as an egg decorator has not been an easy path, but like Arnold Schwarzenegger, what makes me hard to comprehend, unique, and memorable is exactly what has made me successful.

L E S S O N   8 4

Stay with the process.

I continually need to remind myself to stay with the process. The tool I use to draw on my eggs needs to be regularly filled with beeswax. I often resent stopping to fill the small well with chips of wax because I'm enjoying the drawing so much.

This is what happens when I forget to refuel the tool. I begin to notice that the wax lines I'm laying on the egg are getting just the slightest bit scratchy, or some small dirt particles are showing up in the lines. These are indications that the tool is running low on wax—like when I'm driving my car and the refueling light goes on. I never want to stop and fill up. I'd rather just keep on going.

However, both are vital to my progress and process. Once my drawing tool is refilled, I feel free, and I have a renewed sense of purpose. The minor break has refreshed me. The stop at the gas station reminds me that I have to take a break. And I can now use the energy I had lost in checking that gas gauge or wax supply, and my mind and imagination are freed up for the creative task at hand.

L E S S O N   8 5

What at first seems to be a humorous coincidence can be interpreted as a sign from the universe.

For years my universe revolved around me. I was the cause for rain at Shea Stadium when my husband had tickets to see the Mets. My harsh words to my daughter caused her best friend not to invite her to sleep over. I was responsible for everyone and everything. When I finally learned that I wasn't, it was an enormous relief. And I began to think the coincidences might possibly be the work of my higher power.

There was one coincidence that made me laugh out loud. I have become conscientious about writing down every bit of money coming in and going out both for my personal and my business accounts. It's sometimes a nuisance. What I've learned, however, is that attention to detail gets the rewards, so I faithfully record every cent that crosses my path. I received a fifty-dollar gift certificate to a large bookstore, spent forty dollars of it in one shopping expedition, and was given a credit memo for ten dollars. In the car I began puzzling over how to record that debit and credit. It began to feel like too much work. I rationalized that I shouldn't have to record the money from the gift at all. I deliberated some more. I became lost while I was doing all this reflecting. Then, as if from the beyond, Gary Puckett and The Union Gap's song playing on my car radio floated into my consciousness. "Woman. Woman, have you got cheating on your mind?"

L E S S O N   8 6

The rewards offered by taking a leadership role far outweigh the demands of the position.

My father was vice president of Stern Brothers, a department store in New York City. I considered him vice-president of all he and I surveyed, and as daughter of the vice president I was content to serve as second in command, advising the leader and being the trusted servant. In school I ran for secretary or vice president rather than president, stage manager rather than director, helper rather than leader of the troops. I was afraid to bear the full responsibility for being the boss. As long as my superior would take the heat while praising me amply, basking in reflected glory was as much as I could handle.

This is how I changed. The volunteer coordinator at my children's elementary school recognized my artistic talents and asked me to chair the holiday craft and merchandise fair, the biggest fundraising event the school scheduled. She was someone I admired and knew I would enjoy working with her. I knew she would support me in the work. So at thirty-three, I said yes to a leadership role for the first time in my life.

I found that I enjoyed being in charge, being the decision maker. When the family room—the area in the building devoted to volunteers—was abuzz with workers preparing products for the fair, I was in my glory. I doled out assignments, supervised quality control, worked on the budget, and dealt with problems. It was a step toward leadership, but I wouldn't have taken the job on without the coordinator's support.

It took me a full year before I took on a leadership role without any support. Years of therapy later on helped me abdicate the role of the chief's key woman. I was ready to be top banana. And in 1996 I accepted the nomination to become the president of the Entrepreneurial Woman's Network, a 300-member organization.

The yearlong commitment was enormous. I led a board of directors consisting of twenty-four women who owned their own businesses. The work was intense, filled with deadlines for workshops, lunches, and roundtable meetings. In addition, I wrote a regular column for the organization's newsletter, presided over the monthly membership luncheons, and dealt with all the issues that arose.

What I loved best was the intensity of the job and interacting with people. It made feel enormously alive, vital. During that year the media called me frequently for comment. I was invited to attend conferences as a representative of the group. Everyone in the organization knew my name. It was never quite like that when I was just a vice president. In that position, I could go and hide. When you're the leader, they come and find you.

Being president that year changed my life and showed me the passion of leadership. I had been president, a claim I could never have made before. And, as long as the Entrepreneurial Woman's Network exists, my name will be listed among the presidents.

CHAPTER 9

Support

"Did you make all these yourself?" the customer would ask while pointing to my display of eggs and jewelry. That question seemed patronizing and demeaning, as if it wasn't possible I could produce the quality or quantity of these goods. At that time, I was doing everything myself and felt I deserved recognition. These days, hardly anyone asks if I do everything myself. And, if they did, my response would be, "No, and I'm proud I don't." I have a few women who help me create my products. In addition, I have legions of support from friends, colleagues, a mastermind group, a success team, a networking group, several associations, a coach, and a loving family. I consider all of their help and encouragement essential to my productivity.

LESSON 87

Find people who can guide you toward your destiny.

I'm sure that some lucky folks out there knew from day one that they were going to be doctors, poets, or presidents. But for the rest of us, it helps to have friends who can guide us. I bumped into two mentors in college. We were required to take a variety of general education courses for a well-rounded liberal arts education. Among these general education requirements were eight credits in the arts. I selected classes in studio art and theater.

In an introductory theater course I met Oliver Allyn, the department chair and stage design professor. After I'd been working backstage painting scenery for several weeks, the professor took me aside, placed his hand on my shoulder, and said, "I'd like to proselytize you. I want you to become a theater arts major." I didn't know how to react. Should I be insulted or pleased? Once he explained his intentions, I went back to my dorm to ponder the invitation. Looking back on that experience, I can see it was the first time I remember any adult, other than my parents and my second-grade art teacher (who used to take me out of class to paint murals), taking an interest in my talents and me. I declared a double major of studio art and theater.

Jim Cavanaugh arrived in the theater department my senior year. He was well known in his field as a director. He made me property mistress for his first production on campus, The Caucasian Chalk Circle. As an upperclassman, I thought the job was beneath me until I read the script and discovered that there were well over one hundred props to collect and create including Bunraku (Japanese-style) puppets and an imaginary river.

He also invited me to design the logo for the production. He scheduled a trip to the printers and accompanied me to their offices. The printer handed me a sheet of typefaces and asked me to select fonts and point sizes. Huh? In 1969 this was Greek to me. I looked at Jim for his opinion, but he refused to intervene. "You're the designer, Jane."

He challenged me by making me responsible for major decisions that could make or break the show. His generosity was monumental to me as an emerging artist and entrepreneur. His trust that I could deliver a superior product helped me respect myself as an artist.

L E S S O N   8 8

Set aside childhood behaviors
that impede your success.

Forty-five women sat on the floor of an exercise studio, mirrors all around. One by one they shared intimate details of their lives, and it became clear that each had used relationships to fill a gaping hole inside of them. Although I didn't share anything with them for several months, I recognized that this was a place where I would feel comfortable. It marked the beginning of a transformation that affected my career, personal growth, and success.

For the first time, I began to address issues that had held me back in my life and ultimately, in my work. I am not a psychologist and do not pretend that I am an expert in addictive behavior. But I am an entrepreneur who understands the enormous impact of personal dysfunction in a business. I have become part of a fellowship that offers practical, spiritual-based tools for managing my life. By using these tools daily, I have been able to set aside behaviors that impeded my success. I transformed myself from a shy young woman hiding behind an artistic gift to a mature adult who is willing to take her place in the world based on her talents, intelligence, and drive.

Eliminating my addictive behaviors helped me uncover the motivation behind most of my actions. When I become keenly and often uncomfortably aware of why I am behaving a certain way, I am more likely to change that behavior and do the right thing. When I was in an addictive mode, I would use a substance (sugar), a person (a phone call), or an action (procrastinating) to alleviate any discomfort a situation created. Today I no longer medicate feelings. I experience the pain and analyze why I'm feeling it. Then I move swiftly and directly to deal with its cause.

For instance, I never used to question a rejection or investigate why it happened. I simply figured I wasn't good enough. Now when I get a rejection, I take a moment to breathe and reflect on what I can learn from it. With the support of a coach, I will request five minutes of time from the decision maker to inquire what I might do to increase my chances in the future, what criteria I didn't meet. or anything else that may have factored into the rejection. The response always teaches me something. Most important, however, is that I am no longer afraid to address an authority figure—a fear that held me back for too many years.

My personal transformation had a significant effect on the lives of four other people as well, the four people most important to me— my husband and children. Several years ago, when Lindsey, Robert, and Laura were all living at home, we had five different sets of needs. I called a family meeting and asked everyone to bring date books or calendars. We sat in our living room and each of us discussed our upcoming events for the next month. The goal was to be supportive of each other, and to make sure we knew who needed which car. When I described this forum to my counselor he said, "Do you know what we call that?" I was sure he was going to say "anal," but his answer surprised and delighted me. "Functional." I couldn't have asked for higher praise.

LESSON 89

A mastermind group can help you develop to the point where you can afford luxuries with or without a tax write-off.

For years I'd been trying to figure out how to go to a luxury spa and write the trip off as a business expense. Many business conferences are held at great locations, hotels, and resorts. Those business trips are fully deductible for the participants. Why couldn't I take an expensive trip to some luxurious locale and work on strategic planning with a group of advisers? My accountant informed me that as long as the trip was business-related—and could be documented as such—then it would be an acceptable tax deduction. I decided that somehow, someday, I would figure out a way to go to a Golden Door or Canyon Ranch and get a tax write-off. Greed can work for you when you're an entrepreneur.

In the mid 1990s, I got together a support group for my business that is still going strong. I invited several of my entrepreneurial friends to my home for a brainstorming session. I wanted to form a mastermind group that would meet monthly *and* take an annual spa retreat for the purpose of professional development and business planning. Mastermind groups were mentioned on the audiotapes I listened to regularly. The group consists of hand-chosen business advisers from different industries who meet regularly to focus on one another's businesses.

Our six-member NYCONN group (members from New York and Connecticut) meets twelve times a year, usually on the third Monday of each month. We gather at one of our homes at 6:00 P.M. and have the same menu of Chinese take-out so that food is not an issue. Conversation over dinner is social. At 6:30 P.M. we begin going around the circle, focusing on each member's business for a specified amount of time.

The advantages of this association are profound. For one thing, once a month I know that I am accountable to five other people for what I have accomplished in the previous month. Our format requires each of us to set goals monthly. At the beginning of the session, we each talk about the outcomes of the previous month's goals.

The second round is to focus on challenges—what's giving us difficulty in the workplace. I've used my focus time to try out a new speech or to ask for input on suggestions for a book I was writing, while others discuss employee issues, burnout, or frustration over rejections.

The next and final round is to set goals for the following meeting. As the goal-setting monitor, I always force members to make sure their goals are realistic and specific. We also make sure that those goals required more effort than activities that a member would accomplish anyway. Attending a monthly association meeting is not a goal, while traveling to the Toy Fair in Nuremberg is.

In addition to having the opportunity to talk about my business with other professionals, I get to hear what's going on in other fields. I feel less isolated, get a larger worldview, and have my efforts validated by business owners I respect.

We've had several celebrations as goals are reached, including a dinner treat at a local restaurant when the owner of a gift business hired a new sales rep, and a gourmet meal when a member secured another backer for her organization.

The spa trip hasn't happened yet, although I can tell it's closer to reality. It's great to have a goal for us to work toward as a group. My dream was big, a tax-deductible spa vacation. The irony is that I achieved a truly bigger goal, a functional support group.

LESSON 90

A fail-safe method to move toward a goal: promising a colleague you will accomplish a challenging task within a specified time.

In my first book, I wanted to illustrate the phenomenon that occurs with the aniline dyes I use to color my egg designs. Dye sequencing is a curious part of my craft. I knew it would be informative and visually compelling for readers. Yet I couldn't discipline myself to sit down and figure out a way to treat this project in text and photos. I kept saving it for later, and the deadline for my book was rapidly approaching.

One afternoon I sat next to a talented florist at an Entrepreneurial Woman's Network event.

The speaker's topic that day was committing yourself to a goal. She asked us each to share an undertaking we had been putting off. My partner, the florist, had her own task she had been avoiding. I told her mine. We had taken the first step toward making our goals real.

On my way home I stopped at the grocery store to pick up five-dozen eggs. I was so charged with my mission I couldn't wait to get home. Once there, I started to work on the dye-sequencing technique. I recorded the egg-dyeing process, noting each step along the way. Then I created a chart that identified how each of the different colors was achieved, the amount of time the egg remained in each dye bath, and in what order the dyes were used. I needed motivation and accountability, and the florist's interest in my task and description of hers was enough to get me going. Nearly ten years later I still remember the power of this first experience. I know someone out there is aware of my challenge. I feel encouraged to report back the results of my work, knowing that I will receive approval for working on it.

For the chart in my book, I ultimately dyed over sixty eggs to demonstrate what happens with different dye combinations. Readers frequently compliment me on this section in my book. However, doing the job was more valuable to me than it was to them.

LESSON 91

Ask for informational support and also emotional support.

Growing up, I was advised by my peers never to admit I didn't know something. I interpreted this to mean that I should never ask questions. The overriding message was that I shouldn't appear stupid. So I took part only in things I was familiar with. Furthermore, I despised those people who had the stupidity to admit they didn't know something. My disgust was compounded when the offender publicly asked for answers. How could they? One day I realized that those silly people who were asking all those dumb questions were getting a whole lot further ahead in life than I was. When I began changing my attitude, I was amazed that no one said I was stupid.

There were two sides of my problem. Not only did I hate to ask for help, I had difficulty helping anyone. I believed if I shared my knowledge, my information store would be diminished, so I shelled out facts like a miser giving alms. Most people were delighted when someone asked them for help. I marveled at their willingness to expose their vulnerability. I also noticed how generous other people were when I called them for information. I began to notice how flattered I became when someone called me to ask if a craft show was worth attending, what database program I used, or if I could recommend a bookkeeper.

I had the opportunity to put asking for help to an extreme test. An executive outplacement company had invited me to speak to its candidates about entrepreneurship. I had a couple of months to prepare. I was looking forward to helping these ex-executives see the benefits of having their own enterprises. Two weeks before the engagement, I called several of them to ask about their expectations and needs. Although they had been corporate employees, many had acted like entrepreneurs as part of their jobs—managing acquisitions and mergers. The talent I discovered in the audience intimidated me. Two days before the event I wanted to drop out.

Because I'd learned to show up no matter what, I realized this wouldn't be an option. But what could I do? I asked for help. I called my friend Patty who had arranged this speaking engagement. She told me, "Jane, I picked you because you have made a business out of something entirely unthinkable. Who else could tell these guys about being an entrepreneur?" I called my friend, Steve—a business coach. "You're not going to tell them the 'how' or the 'what.' Your strength is in demonstrating the 'who' of entrepreneurship." In total, I called fourteen friends and colleagues. Each filled in a piece of why I had agreed to give the talk in the first place. I made the decision to show up.

When the candidates assembled that Thursday morning, we introduced ourselves. In the audience was a professor from a local college who taught entrepreneurship. "I'm here to keep you honest, Jane," he said with a smile and a wink. Now, I thought, I'm in deep trouble. But he supported everything I said, including my response to one earnest participant who asked if a start-up should hire all the professionals he needed right away—lawyers, accountants, etc. "In my experience," I shared, "I hired as needed. When a legal issue arose, I found a lawyer."

The college professor nodded approvingly. The ex-executives loved my stories of tenacity and success, and they got my message: entrepreneurship is a satisfying lifestyle decision that has its trials and tribulations like any other form of business. Their smiles and relaxed postures showed me that they recognized and appreciated the joy I feel in my work.

That morning, my biggest achievement was walking through the door of the conference room to face my fear and deliver my message. The other reward came when one of the candidates came up to me afterward. He had been an executive with a major Wall Street banking firm.

"I've always had a dream of becoming an artist. You have reawakened that possibility for me. Thank you." My willingness to set aside my false pride and ask for help was doubly rewarded that day.

Articulating your plan to a sympathetic person makes it easier to begin doing it.

"If you don't hear from me within a half hour, you may need to send an ambulance to my house." I was talking to my friend Pat because I needed some bolstering. I was planning to call the gift buyer at Neiman Marcus, and my heart was beating so fast, it scared me. Having another soul out there who knows and cares about me and what I'm about to do, someone I can talk to, has been a godsend. Also, once I've committed myself to make the move and told a sympathetic friend or colleague, there's no backing out.

Immediately after I hung up the phone, I dialed the Neiman Marcus headquarters in Dallas. I got the buyer's voice mail. What a relief! I'd followed through on my commitment without having to actually speak to the buyer. Voicemail also let me hear the buyer's disembodied voice so I developed a mental image of her. I also learned when it would be convenient for me to try again. I was thrilled that I had taken this first step. I knew it would be much easier to call the next time. I had gotten my feet wet. Wading in up to my knees would be that much simpler. I called Pat back to share my excitement. Bookending is a term I've borrowed from Alcoholics Anonymous. A book cannot stand upright easily. It needs support on each side by other books. Books are not unlike people. In AA you are encouraged to take risks with the aid of another concerned member of the organization. Bookending gives home office workers what the water cooler provides in corporations—a place to find support.

It works reciprocally, too. While it was helpful for me to know that I could call Pat and bookend my fears, it also helps when I'm the recipient of a call. One day Pat called me when she decided to master the electronic keyboard she had recently purchased," I'm vowing to go through the instruction book page by page and not take any shortcuts." Pat said she'd spend the next two hours reading through the manual. She inspired me. I had recently purchased a digital camera I assumed I should know how to use. Her example motivated me to study the instruction pamphlet, a step I often skip. I was also honored that she trusted me enough to reveal that she, too, was mortal and did not to know how to do everything perfectly the first time.

L E S S O N   9 3

Hiring a coach for a month or a year is a worthwhile investment.

On our Tuesday morning walks at Compo Beach, Alicia and I talk about our families and our lives, but mostly we talk about our businesses. She owns a travel agency that provides customized tours. For weeks she kept referring to a woman called Valerie, who seemed to be important to her company. When I finally asked her who Valerie was, she said, "Valerie is a member of the The International Coaching Federation." She suggested that I add at least three clients to my roster this quarter as a way of increasing revenues without overselling my current clients. I've been cruising the Internet looking for organizations in New England that I haven't approached yet about my garden tours." I finally met Valerie at an Entrepreneurial Woman's Network event a few months later. We made a phone appointment for a trial coaching session.

My way of doing business changed dramatically after I began working with Valerie, but I can't explain exactly what she does or how she does it. At first, I attempted to analyze her method, her questions, and her responses—for about five minutes. Then the process took over and I became so engrossed in self-exploration that I forgot to pay attention to what Valerie was doing.

She guided me through the development of the Circle of Life collection—my dozen eggs in a glass carton. What started as the brainchild of Faith Ringgold in June 1998 was brought to fruition at the New York Gift Show in August 2000. It was Valerie who fanned the flames as my own enthusiasm dampened following disappointment after disappointment. She was there to listen, encourage, and nudge me onward. She also suggested that I record every step of the journey, because it would make a great speech or book one day.

In addition, when my enthusiasm flagged, Valerie asked me probing questions. She helped me uncover hidden feelings from my earliest childhood that had kept me emotionally handicapped and prevented me from moving forward. I used to think that maybe I was the only one who suffered from the bondage of early behavior patterns, until I read an article in the business section of *The New York Times* about two real estate moguls who were fighting over a piece of property. One of them bid a ridiculously high amount for a building simply because he didn't want the other guy to have it. Talk about childhood issues. Who doesn't need to examine their behaviors?

Hiring a coach is a smart move for soul proprietors, executives, or anyone interested in moving forward in life.

This is the way coaching works, as defined on the International Coach Federation web site:

> *Professional Coaching is an ongoing partnership that helps clients produce fulfilling results in their personal and professional lives. Through the process of coaching, clients deepen their learning, improve their performance, and enhance their quality of life. In each meeting, the client chooses the focus of conversation, while the coach listens and contributes observations and questions. This interaction creates clarity and moves the client into action. Coaching accelerates the client's progress by providing greater focus and awareness of choice. Coaching concentrates on where clients are today and what they are willing to do to get where they want to be tomorrow.*

Part of Valerie's success as my coach is that she taught me to ask myself the questions she would pose. I can always call her for a check-in, but I am not dependent upon her to run my business. She empowered me to understand my own motives, behaviors, and fears so that I could recognize and deal with them.

CHAPTER 10

Lessons from the Masters

During my career I have met a few extraordinary people who have inspired and encouraged me along the entrepreneurial road. They are my beacons as I forge ahead. I used to be uncomfortable receiving such help without being able to return the favor. I was reared on the instant-reciprocation model. But how could I repay those people who had led the way for me? When Lindsey was born, a friend gave me two cartons filled with adorable outfits and accessories that her children had outgrown. Because her kids were older, I knew that she wouldn't need them returned. But I had to ask how I could repay her generosity. And she said simply, "Pass it on." It has become my mission to do so.

LESSON 94

Translate the success of someone you admire into realistic goals.

Shortly after college graduation Lindsey, my oldest child, attended a goal-setting workshop I gave and was stumped by the assignment. She didn't know what direction she wanted to take in her life and told me, "I'm not sure how to make this a goal, but I know I'd like to be the next Anna Quindlen." Having someone you admire is a good yardstick in setting a goal. Lindsey needed to figure out what it was about Anna Quindlen that appealed to her, and then she had to work backward to determine what steps it would take to get there.

"What is it about Anna Quindlen that you admire?" I asked her. "She wrote those great columns in The New York Times, and now she's a novelist."

"There are lots of journalists and writers out there. What particularly appeals to you about Anna Quindlen?" "Her columns speak to me as a woman."

"What else?" "I like that she's married and has kids."

"Anything else?" "I'm impressed by her willingness to give up her job at the Times to be with her kids and write novels."

Working this way, Lindsey was able to extract a set of goals for herself. She could transform Anna Quindlen's attributes—working for the Times, appealing to a female audience, and having a family she's committed to—into small chunks in order to form long term goals. Lindsey had to do the following:

- Find out how to write for *The New York Times*.

- Write and submit articles about experience as a college student.

- Continue dating as a precursor to choosing a husband and having a family.

It's smart to choose a role model you can adopt. Who wouldn't like to have the genius of Bill Gates, the leadership of Gloria Steinem, the culinary talents of Julia Child, the kindness and generosity of Mother Teresa, and the looks of Elizabeth Hurley or Mel Gibson? If we try to put together an unrealistic combination of talents, we defeat the possibility of ever measuring up.

By selecting Anna Quindlen, a real human being, Lindsey doesn't need to worry about her role model's fashion expertise or technological wizardry. She can focus on the elements that are important to her: family values and writing skills.

My role models continually change. In my early career in crafts, my model was Linda Carr, who brought her curly-haired daughter to work at craft shows with her and was sought as a designer by Vogue Patterns. Now my model and mentor is Rosita Perez, a wife and mother who several years ago at age forty transformed her career from social worker to one of the country's most successful keynote speakers.

LESSON 95

The success story of someone who has traveled the route before you can help you stay the course.

Charna Garber, the president of a luxury shoe manufacturing company, was the keynote speaker at my Entrepreneurial Woman's Network luncheon. She described her first trip to Italy to meet the foreman of the leather shop that would produce her company's shoes. It was not only her first time in that country, it was also her first experience driving a car with manual transmission. As she jerked back and forth along the highway on her way to meet a stranger in a strange land, she thought, "What am I doing here? What have I gotten myself into?" It got worse. When she arrived at the factory, Tony, the foreman, was shocked that the new president of the shoe company was a woman. He turned his back on her, saying he wouldn't work with her. Because she didn't have any options other than getting back into the rental car, she stood up to him. "You at least have to give me a chance." He did. When she reported her story to us, their relationship was well into its second decade.

I was on my way to exhibit my work at a craft show in Boston one snowy Thursday morning in December. I had racks on top of my van and a carload of display pieces and merchandise. The snow was falling heavily. My car was swerving back and forth, and I wasn't sure where the thruway entrance was. Tears started streaming down my cheeks. All I wanted was to be home by a fire, snuggled up under a quilt with a good novel. But I wasn't. And I didn't turn back. Instead, I thought of Charna Garber.

These are the moments when I use prayer. Otherwise, my head becomes filled with negative thoughts, and I do believe we bring into our lives what we think about. So I said a prayer—several times, and the moment passed. The show was a success, and the storm became a badge of honor in my entrepreneurial rucksack.

I realize that not everything is going to be easy. To achieve success, there will be uncomfortable, even scary moments. A friend once said in reference to raising our children that as long as the general direction is forward, it's good.

L E S S O N 9 6

Even when copycats threaten your livelihood, keep doing what you do best.

I couldn't believe my eyes. I was just about to ask, "Where's Linda?" when I finally found my friend's exhibit in the maze of colorful merchandise spread across the Guilford Green. On closer inspection, though, I realized it wasn't Linda's booth at all. The dolls looked a lot like Linda's, but something was missing. They didn't touch me the way Linda's had.

Before I met her I was struck by the display she had created for her work. I had attended my first Guilford Handcrafts Expo—the granddaddy of craft shows—to see if becoming a craft artist was for me. Linda and I became friends a year later at the Westport Handcrafts Fair (my first crafts show) when she offered to trade her dolls for my eggs.

In her Guilford booth, Linda's products hung from swings, sat on diminutive rocking chairs, or posed in other lifelike stances. The boy and girl dolls were dressed in Oshkosh overalls; the young maidens in fine Italian-cotton print dresses. Their embroidered faces and hair made of yarn turned them into children you wanted to take home. Her competitor, at the booth I had mistakenly thought was hers, had displayed her dolls in exactly the same poses as Linda's, copied their outfits, their expressions, the fabrics, and the labels.

When I told her about the person who was imitating her dolls, I was impressed with how she handled the situation. Rather than kick and scream to the show management, as I might have done, Linda saved her energy. She invented new designs, spent quality time with her customers, and ignored her rival until she disappeared a year or two later.

Ironically, a few years later, a customer accused Linda of copying another person's designs. Linda told the misinformed Samaritan with a gentle smile, "I'm not copying anyone. I'm the person who designs these dolls for Vogue."

L E S S O N   9 7

Whether your audience is one person or a thousand, speak as though they are your most important clients.

When I considered attending a seminar on business law, it looked about as exciting as reading the encyclopedia. I knew I could get some interesting information out of it if I delved, but who wanted to make the effort? However, it was a requirement for the business owner's course I was taking with the American Women's Economic Development Corporation. So I dragged myself into New York City to attend the first session.

But, even though it was required, I was the only member of my class to show up. Still, instructor Jill Botway spoke as if I was the most important client or audience she had ever addressed. Her session was riveting. Jill was a brilliant, successful attorney whose legal team had never lost a case. What I remember most about her session, now nearly a decade later, was the story she told about the Mianus Bridge which collapsed near my home. The bridge is on a span of Interstate 95, a highly trafficked artery in the Northeast. It was unthinkable that a piece of a major highway could simply cave in. It caused hideous traffic congestion until repairs were finished a year later.

Jill was the lawyer for the woman whose car had plunged into the Mianus River when the road fell away. As Jill capsulized the issue, "When you're pushing a wheelchair holding your twenty-three-year-old client into the courtroom and it's her against the big business contractors who built the bridge, she's going to win the sympathy of the court." The case, which ended with a negotiated settlement, produced the largest award in Connecticut's history at that time.

Later, when not one soul showed up for a class I was scheduled to conduct in a store, it was Jill's professionalism at the seminar that I remembered. I did the right thing. I invited the manager to round up any employees who might be interested in the material and presented my talk to them. Without Jill's model, I might have behaved in a different way—I might have complained to the owner of the store about her store's advertising campaign or let my disappointment show to my new audience, the employees who decided to attend.

It is possible to continue doing the work you love for as long as you like.

It was an opportunity I couldn't refuse. I got a call from a producer at "The Carol Duvall Show" asking if a crew could come and do a story on me, a field show, they called it. Craft artists are sometimes videotaped in their studios discussing and demonstrating what they do. They asked if I would follow it up with a visit to their television studio in Burbank, California. Multiple appearances on national television sounded like a very good idea until I started making the arrangements.

To make the trip airplane affordable, my publisher, who was paying my fare, asked that I spend a Saturday night in Burbank to save some money. Because my brother and his family live in Los Angeles, I knew I could stay with him, and I agreed. Also, I realized it was an opportunity to combine business with pleasure. However, I knew I would lose five working days by going. Would it be worth it?

WIIFM—the acronym for "what's in it for me"—is a question business owners are constantly asking when opportunities arise. Although the allure of being on national television is thrilling, using precious workdays can be questionable. Net-net, what was the benefit to this artist? The answer to that was simple: Carol Duvall.

Having a role model like Carol Duvall is an inspiration. She's twenty years my senior and still going strong. She's feisty, smart, and down-to-earth. Her excellent crew, who are devoted to her, help her reach millions of Americans twice daily on HGTV.

I met Carol in the early 1990s in Philipsburg, New Jersey, during the twentieth anniversary of a craft show called the Eggsibit. Carol was with "The Home Show" at the time, a network program starring Gary Collins that included her five-minute craft portion. She was cruising the Eggsibit with her camera crew recording footage of the event. They stopped by my display for an interview and comments, recording my work, among others, for future TV audiences to see. I was immediately attracted to Carol with her bright red eyeglasses and her no-nonsense approach. So, as she and the camera crew finished taping my booth, I asked her if she would be available for dinner. When the other artists saw us leave the hall together later that day, they probably wondered how I got so lucky. I simply asked her. Just asking for what I want is one key to my success as an entrepreneur.

Before I flew out to California, I asked the producer if she could arrange a dinner for Carol and me. Fortunately, Carol's schedule permitted her to leave the set at a reasonable hour, and we had a wonderful time catching up on each other's careers. We also discussed how she might use my services in the future. I ended up with an opportunity to provide a paid, hands-on experience for Carol's entire staff and their families. That workshop was videotaped and aired as well.

The major economic benefit to spending all that time traveling and taping was the boost in sales that it gave my first book. An even greater benefit is getting to work with someone like Carol, to observe her in her milieu, and to have her become an advocate for my business.

LESSON 99

There is much to learn from your corporate friends.

I've never regretted my lack of corporate experience. It seems like a foreign land to me. I know a lot of people who have visited there, some who've even stayed for a while. But for me, it's always been an exotic place from which I have received only souvenirs.

I went from graduate school directly into teaching in the public school system. When I was in college, going to business school was considered a step down from the liberal arts way of life so highly regarded in the late 1960s and early 1970s.

My contacts with corporate types were few and far between—the husbands of friends and one college roommate who hated it but stayed anyway. One night my husband and I had dinner with a Fortune Fifty employee acquaintance. As we were touring his home, I admired his large Edward Steichen print of Greta Garbo. "Yeah, they wouldn't let me hang that at the office, 'Too distracting.'"

You know how we form judgments quickly and indelibly? I heard that piece of information and later another about women in corporate offices not being allowed to wear dangling earrings—also distracting—and I was forever anti-corporate. Of course, this is more a reflection of my judgmental attitude than it was about corporate culture. I used to think in black and white terms only. It was easier for me to dismiss the entire corporate structure, based on anecdotal information, than to accept their policies as functional for that kind of productivity. Today, I've come to admire the training and expertise exhibited by the growing number of formerly corporate people who have become my friends.

My lack of corporate training amuses them as I gape at their simplest knowledge.

I was having lunch with my friend Gigi one afternoon. We were, as always, discussing our businesses. I was describing the holiday ornaments that I create each Christmas season. They are by far my best sellers, always completely sold out by the end of the year. "Your cash cows," she remarked. I got the visual image right away: something that keeps producing and becomes a main stream of revenue for a business. I thought Gigi was a genius for coming up with such a clever phrase and I told her so. "Jane," she said. "Every company has a cash cow. At General Mills (where she had been employed) it was Cheerios. We're always trying to find a new cash cow."

I felt as though I was living on a different planet because I had never heard that phrase. Because this has happened to me several times, I began to read the business section of the newspaper on a more regular basis.

When a member of my mastermind group asked if a particular speaker I knew had been "vetted," I felt that similar surge of embarrassment because I had never heard that word before although I vaguely knew its essence. My husband had never encountered the phrase "glass ceiling." That's understandable. He teaches in a school that has such a high predominance of women teachers, there's no need for that phrase.

There is much for me to learn from my corporate friends. And, as corporations are now learning, entrepreneurs have much to offer them as well.

LESSON 100

Heed the advice of those who have gone before you. It's a good way to avoid mistakes.

When an NSA colleague, Nancy Stevens, referred me for an opportunity to be a keynote speaker for a group in Argentina, I knew there would be many hurdles I'd have to leap over. For one thing I had never addressed such a large audience before. Nor had I ever had to speak for such a long period of time. I also was told I had to adapt my materials to a PC platform, and as a die-hard Macintosh owner, this was the most daunting part of the job.

I approached this assignment with more diligence than I had ever applied to any task. First I signed up for a PowerPoint class at a local training center. There were fifteen students in the class, all of whom were using PCs. I was the only one using a Mac, and the instructor was distinctly annoyed when I kept interrupting him to ask questions. But in time I was able to master the computer program and use PowerPoint.

However, there were more problems. When I tell the story of my business, I illustrate my talk with slides of my work, using a carousel projector. I had to convert all those transparencies to a CD-Rom so I could import them into PowerPoint. So I had to work with a computer guru who walked me through that process. I now had a complete PowerPoint presentation on my Mac. My techno-genius was then able to convert the Mac disk into a PC one and send it to Argentina.

In addition to the computer coursework, I began talking to colleagues about my forthcoming trip abroad. Nancy Stevens and others recommended a book on cultural differences called Kiss, Bow or Shake Hands, which I read carefully. I also had tea with a woman from Buenos

Aires in order to check out some of my stories—I wanted to know if my references would be clear to the audience I would soon be addressing. For instance, would they understand what I meant by the White House? And would it be acceptable for me to use slang? Most important—my friends gave me one piece of advice repeatedly. They told me to bring along my own computer, just in case anything went wrong with my plan.

I was required to send my PowerPoint seminar on disk to Argentina ahead of time so that the organization sponsoring the seminar would be able to print it out and give copies to the members of the audience.

I looked into renting a PC for the trip, but the cost was not reasonable. I ultimately made the decision to abandon the Macintosh and buy a new PC, and I was able to get up to speed on Windows software before I boarded the plane to South America in April, 1998. I ultimately used my own PC laptop during the presentation and was glad I made the decision and spent the money.

I was happy and eager to do whatever was necessary. And all the legwork required for the venture paid off—it was a thrill being hailed as an internationally known speaker.

LESSON 101

Truly understanding your core values
will make some choices easier to refuse.

"Save your red lights." I remember the advice I heard at a parenting group many years ago. "If you say no to too many things, your children won't recognize when your no really means something. You only get so many red lights." I decided that my red lights would be used to prevent poor grades, substance abuse, and teen pregnancy. Eating too many Halloween treats or staying up past bedtime playing video games were not going to be issues I badgered my kids about.

Similarly, defining what is and is not okay for my entrepreneurial life has helped me recognize my core values:

- Having time for the people I care about.

- Feeling valued for what I do.

- Keeping my life uncomplicated.

So I flashed red lights at opportunities that would interfere with those choices. When my children were young, I did not participate in activities that required a lot of travel. I simply did not put myself into arenas that would prevent me from taking care of my children.

One October, after my children were grown, I received a phone inquiry that tested my values. A high-ranking executive had received one of my custom-designed eggs as a present from a client. She was so delighted she wanted to hire me to create a gift for each of the corporation's key employees.

My cranial cash register began feverishly calculating the possibilities. I thought it would be not only workable but also profitable to fit one or two dozen extra $300 pieces into my production schedule. "About how many gifts would that be?" I inquired. "We'd need a thousand," she replied. "And our budget would allow for $30–35 per gift." A $35,000 budget! How could I help this woman!? I asked her for twenty-four hours to consider her offer.

In that price range I would be able to provide my lowest-cost item, holiday ornaments. To make them unique to the receivers I would add the company logo to the design and personalize each one with the employee's name.

I began mentally lining up other egg decorators I knew and calculating the cost of subcontracting. I calculated the time it would take to negotiate with each one. I considered the systems I'd need to develop for purchasing plus packing and shipping such an enormous order. I visualized this executive's thousand employees opening up their gifts and what their reactions would be. I didn't like what I saw. My art form requires a unique audience. Not everyone loves what I do, nor appreciates the heart and soul that go into the making of each piece. I know that good whiskey takes years to reach perfection, but I wouldn't appreciate receiving it as a gift even if it had my name written on it. My visualization captured the picture of several confused recipients dangling their ornaments quizzically and saying, "An egg???"

All three of my core values—having time, keeping it simple, and feeling valued—would be challenged by this opportunity. Since my bottom line is not measured in dollars, I said no to the executive.

1 0 1 L E S S O N S

1. Take care of your image, and you will be taken seriously.

2. If you really want something, pursue it directly.

3. Perception is everything. Keep your message clear and consistent.

4. The public needs to place us, and it's our job to make it easy for them.

5. It's best to focus your message carefully in every aspect of your business—written, visual, and operational.

6. It's necessary to dress the part.

7. If you're going to compete in business, your printed materials need to project the statement that you are a serious player.

8. Words shape your company's image. Make sure they reflect what you want said about your business.

9. Get as much mileage as you can from opportunities that arise, but keep it honest.

10. Getting advice from an expert is critical. You'll save time and money.

11. The clarity and direction gained from writing a business plan will give you a solid foundation for your business.

12. Never apologize for organizing your day.

13. Attention to details matters.

14. You don't hurt anyone's feelings when you toss bulk mail.

15. Organizing yourself helps you get to the questions that need answers.

16. When someone gives you a lead, do the necessary work, even though the rewards aren't known in advance.

17. Get comfortable asking about money.

18. Break down the items on your to-do list into manageable pieces.

19. It's your business, and you are in charge of every aspect of it, even the jobs you delegate.

20. Writing down your goals is the beginning of the transformation process.

21. Whenever you receive a compliment, simply say, "Thank you."

22. Before you hire people to provide special services, get a recommendation from a person who is familiar with their abilities.

23. Be open to new encounters. Be careful not to prejudge people.

24. There are always days that are slated for growth or learning. Stay with them and don't get upset.

25. Contact your customers frequently, but don't worry if they don't respond quickly.

26. It's important to know when to discard something you already have for the promise of something better to come.

27. Consider yourself lucky if there are only minor irritations in your day.

28. Occasionally the planets may line up to force you to take time off.

29. It's hell learning how to use new gadgets and new systems, but remember you are not alone.

30. In the long run you learn more from your failures than from your successes.

31. Self pity will get you nowhere. You have to respond to a tough situation directly with action.

32. As you work, continually evaluate what is the next thing you have to do in order to succeed.

33. When someone asks how you got that incredible break, the simple answer is hard work.

34. It's easy to save money by using your time, or to save time by using your money but it's hard to decide which.

35. Tackle today's tasks today. Don't postpone anything that you really have to do.

36. Make a commitment to improve yourself a little bit each day. You'll see the results.

37. Exert control over your own destiny.

38. Take it to the next level. Invest time to create systems for your business that will save time in the future.

39. Keep talking to various experts until you reach the perfect solution.

40. The business plan is not as important as the process of creating it.

41. Create a resume as though you were applying for a job. You'll be impressed by who you are.

42. Driving to the correct conclusion of a problem is marvelous. And it's also wonderful to be recognized for your work.

43. Pursue your goals systematically. You will get where you want to go, but not necessarily the way you planned.

44. Enjoy the ride, but don't let the ride drive you.

45. Realize that the support you get from your family will wax and wane.

46. A sense of humor is helpful in learning humility.

47. There will be things you don't even know that you don't know until they come up.

48. Go! You might meet somebody!

49. Oh yeah, Murphy's Law.

50. Make sure your business suits your ever-changing lifestyle.

51. You have to step out of your comfort zone, take risks, and survive the moments of dread to grow your business.

52. In changing what is into what can be we learn what we need to know.

53. Plowing through the nitty-gritty details to complete each task creates big results.

54. Learn from each experience—positive or negative—and move forward.

55. Time and turnover in your industry will provide opportunities to present the same idea more than once.

56. Until they say, "Never call us again!" Don't give up. Keep calling.

57. Look before you leap to conclusions.

58. Don't quit before the miracle.

59. When you have a problem and have trouble finding an answer, persist in your search. It's worth it.

60. Even experienced professionals get nervous approaching new markets.

61. When you get an inspiration, go for it.

62. Trust the instinct that moved you to write a task on your calendar and follow through with it.

63. As difficult as it is, you can teach yourself to believe you deserve what you charge for your work.

64. Once you're on your own, the only person responsible for your life and well being is you.

65. Step out of your comfort zone when someone asks you to do something that seems hard.

66. When you acknowledge that your childhood feelings are interfering with your business relationships, you can move on.

67. Seeing a friend transformed by illness alters your definition of what a challenge is.

68. To avoid feeling like an impostor, work through all the developmental stages first.

69. Build your reputation one customer at a time.

70. Not every financial outlay will yield visible revenues.

71. Listen to customers' complaints. It will pay off.

72. Constructive feedback from customers will make you a better entrepreneur. Accept it with grace.

73. It is important to thank everyone who has helped you in significant ways.

74. Stay focused on the people who are buying your products.

75. When you show up and do the footwork, the universe clears a path for you.

76. The more ambitious the vision, the more arduous the journey. The harder the journey, the bigger the thrill when it is completed.

77. Trust your gut.

78. What you do for pleasure is your passion.

79. At any given moment, you are doing exactly what you choose to be doing, whether you admit it or not.

80. Success is enjoying what you've worked hard to get and recognizing you're there.

81. Choose the vendors who listen to you.

82. If you are able to pursue your passions, you are among the lucky few.

83. What makes you unique makes you successful.

84. Stay with the process.

85. What at first seems to be a humorous coincidence can be interpreted as a sign from the universe.

86. The rewards offered by taking a leadership role far outweigh the demands of the position.

87. Find people who can guide you toward your destiny.

88. Set aside childhood behaviors that impede your success.

89. A mastermind group can help you develop to the point where you can afford luxuries with or without a tax write-off.

90. A fail-safe method to move toward a goal: promising a colleague you will accomplish a challenging task within a specified time.

91. Ask for informational support and also emotional support.

92. Articulating your plan to a sympathetic person makes it easier to begin doing it.

93. Hiring a coach for a month or a year is a worthwhile investment.

94. Translate the success of someone you admire into realistic goals.

95. The success story of someone who has traveled the route before you can help you stay the course.

96. Even when copycats threaten your livelihood, keep doing what you do best.

97. Whether your audience is one person or a thousand, speak as though they are your most important clients.

98. It is possible to continue doing the work you love for as long as you like.

99. There is much to learn from your corporate friends.

100. Heed the advice of those who have gone before you. It's is a good way to avoid mistakes.

101. Truly understanding your core values will make some choices easier to refuse.

RESOURCES

Adhesive Packaging Specialists—
epoxy packaging
103 Foster Street
Peabody, MA 01960
800.222.1117
www.adhesivepackaging.com

Artoria—hand-painted
porcelain egg boxes
225 Fifth Avenue Suite 919
New York, NY 10010
212.532.4670
800.416.0900
www.artoria.com

American Women's Economic
Development Corp.
(AWED)
216 East 45th Street, 10th Floor
New York, NY 10017
212.692.9100
situfts@aol.com

Valerie Barone—Coach
Reach! Unlimited
www.valeriebarone.com

Beverly Ellsley Interiors
www.beverlyellsley.com

Country Living Magazine
www.countryliving.com

Crafts at the Castle
(Sponsored by Family Services
of Greater Boston)
31 Heath Street
Jamaica Plain, MA 02130
617.523.6400
catc@fsgb.org

The Carol Duvall Show—HGTV
www.hgtv.com

Entrepreneurial Woman's Network
P.O. Box 683
Westport, CT 06881-0683
203.222.3404
www.ewn-ct.org

Fashion Institute of Technology
Seventh Avenue at 27th Street
New York, NY 10001-5992
212.217.7999
www.fitnyc.suny.edu

Flax Art and Design San Francisco
240 Valley Drive
Brisbane, CA 94005-1206
800.343.3529
www.flaxart.com

George Little Management (Gift and
Stationary Shows at Jacob K.
Javits Convention Center)
10 Bank Street
White Plains, NY 10606-1954
800.272.SHOW
www.glmshows.com

Impression Impact
www.impressionimpact.com

International Coach Federation
www.coachfederation.org

Inventors' Group
(List of local groups)
www.inventorsdigest.com

Thomas Mann Jewelry
www.thomasmann.com

National Speakers Association
1500 South Priest Drive
Tempe, AZ 85281
480.968.2552
www.nsaspeaker.org

Nightingale-Conant (Audiotapes)
800.525.9000
www.nightingale.com

Noëlle Spa for Beauty
1100 High Ridge Road
Stamford, CT 06905
203.322.3445

Ornament Magazine
www.ornamentmagazine.com

Paper House Productions
800.255.7316
www.paperhouseproductions.com

Carmine Picarello, Photographer
www.picarellophoto.com

Priority Management
www.prioritymanagement.com

Faith Ringgold
www.faithringgold.com

*Service Corps of Retired Executives—
SCORE*
800.634.0245
www.score.org

Stew Leonard's
100 Westport Avenue
Norwalk, CT 06851
203.847.7214
www.stewleonards.com

Victoria Magazine
800.876.8696
www.victoriamag.com

RECOMMENDED AUDIO CASSETTES

Secrets of Power Negotiating—by Roger Dawson

Choosing Your Own Greatness—by Wayne Dyer

How to Be a No-Limit Person—by Wayne Dyer

The Strangest Secret—by Earl Nightingale

Take Charge of Your Life—by Jim Rohn

How to Master Your Time—by Brian Tracy

The Psychology of Achievement—by Brian Tracy

Professional Impact/Personal Power Series—Dr. Julie White

BOOKS BY THE CROSSING PRESS

50+ and Looking for Love Online
by Barbara Harrison

A comprehensive guide on how and where to look for love and companionship through personal ads in print and online. This book takes the reader step-by-step through the process of picking where to advertise, creating the perfect personal ad, selecting the right way to respond, and managing the first date. The inevitable risks and often surprising rewards are explained, and practical advice from psychologists, advertising experts, Web site managers, and other 50+ singles is also included.

$12.95 • Paper • ISBN 1-58091-042-4

Bedroom Feng Shui
by Clear Englebert

The first feng shui book devoted exclusively to the bedroom, this guide is a true inspiration for anyone wishing to energize and heal the most important room in their home. *Bedroom Feng Shui* provides easy-to-follow instructions for proper placement of furniture and art, choosing wall colors and bed linens, and getting rid of clutter.

$10.95 • Paper • ISBN 1-58091-109-9

Black Holes and Energy Pirates: How to Recognize and Release Them
by Jesse Reeder

Two phenomena that keep people from reaching their natural creative potential are black holes—unconscious patterns, expectations, and beliefs—and energy pirates—the maneuvering and dodging people do to disguise these patterns and beliefs. Recognizing and understanding human energy fields, and how people are sometimes drained by them, is the key to achieving personal and professional fulfillment. Reeder explains how to overcome these personal barriers to heal and create the life of your dreams.

$14.95 • Paper • ISBN 1-58091-048-3

Feng Shui Demystified
by Clear Englebert

A concise, inexpensive guide to the ancient principles of feng shui for the home, office, and garden. Author Clear Englebert explains the differences in feng shui variations and then discusses how to put the art into practice. This guide enables anyone to practice feng shui for a more peaceful and harmonious home environment. The book also includes a separate full-color bagua, one of feng shui's most powerful tools.

$10.95 • Paper • ISBN 1-58091-078-5

BOOKS BY THE CROSSING PRESS

The Herbal Menopause Book:
Herbs, Nutrition, and Other Natural Therapies
by Amanda McQuade Crawford

This comprehensive volume provides dozens of specific herbal remedies and other natural therapies for women facing the health issues that arise in premenopause, menopause, and post menopause.

$16.95 • Paper • ISBN 0-89594-799-4

Inner Radiance, Outer Beauty
by Ambika Wauters

Ambika Wauters encourages women to seek and nurture themselves by dismissing unrealistic images of their bodies. She helps them find their archetype of beauty from within and express their inner awareness by transforming their physical appearance. Includes a 21–day program for regaining health and beauty.

$14.95 • Paper • ISBN 1-58091-080-7

A Little Book of Altar Magic
by D. J. Conway

This third addition to the successful "A Little Book" series shows us how we, sometimes unknowingly, create altars in our daily surroundings. D. J. Conway offers information on the power and use of colors, and the historic and symbolic meaning of the elements, animals, and objects to help us create magical altars in our personal surroundings.

$9.95 • Paper • ISBN 1-58091-052-1

A Little Book of Love Magic
by Patricia Telesco

A cornucopia of lore, magic, and imaginative ritual designed to bring excitement and romance to your life. Patricia Telesco tells us how to use magic to manifest our hopes and dreams for romantic relationships, friendships, family relations, and passions for our work.

$9.95 • Paper • ISBN 0-89594-887-7

A Little Book of Prosperity Magic
by Cynthia Killion

Learn how to fret less about money, create a "joy budget," hone the art of giving, and set goals for a prosperous life. Meditations and affirmations sprinkled throughout the book help you to "think prosperously" anywhere at any time.

$9.95 • Paper • ISBN 1-58091-118-8

BOOKS BY THE CROSSING PRESS

Living Feng Shui: Personal Stories

by Carole J. Hyder

The case study format allows you to see how feng shui can enhance your life and the floor plans allow you to follow the application of feng shui principles. These elements combine to provide a clear concept and appreciation of feng shui.

—Deborah Sures, feng shui consultant and interior designer

$19.95 • Paper • ISBN 1-58091-115-3

The Natural Remedy Book for Women

by Diane Stein

This bestselling, self-help guide to holistic health care includes information on ten different natural healing methods. Remedies from all ten methods are given for fifty common health problems.

$16.95 • Paper • ISBN 0-89594-525-8

On Women Turning Forty: Coming Into Our Fullness

by Cathleen Rountree

These candid interviews and beautiful photographs will inspire all women who are navigating through the mid-life passage. The updated look of this best-selling classic makes it the perfect companion to the later decades of Rountree's series on women.

$16.00 • Paper • ISBN 0-89594-517-7

Wind and Water: Your Personal Feng Shui Journey

by Carole J. Hyder

This book presents feng shui as simple suggestions that can be done on a daily basis— each page will provide information and a corresponding activity. Instead of reading about feng shui, this book will provide an immediate experience of feng shui.

$19.95 • Paper • ISBN 1-58091-050-5

To receive a current catalog from The Crossing Press,
call us toll-free at 1.800.777.1048
or visit our Web site at **www. crossingpress.com**

www.crossingpress.com

BROWSE through the Crossing Press Web site for information on upcoming titles, new releases, and backlist books including brief summaries, excerpts, author information, reviews, and more.

SHOP our store for all of our books and, coming soon, unusual, interesting, and hard-to-find sideline items related to Crossing's best-selling books!

READ informative articles by Crossing Press authors on all of our major topics of interest.

SIGN UP for our e-mail newsletter to receive late-breaking developments and special promotions from The Crossing Press.